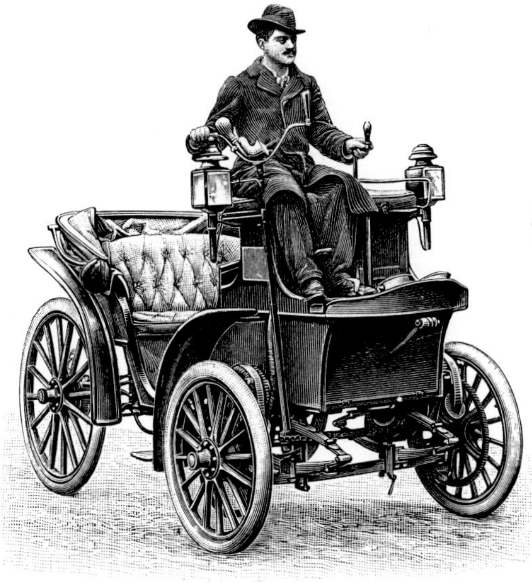

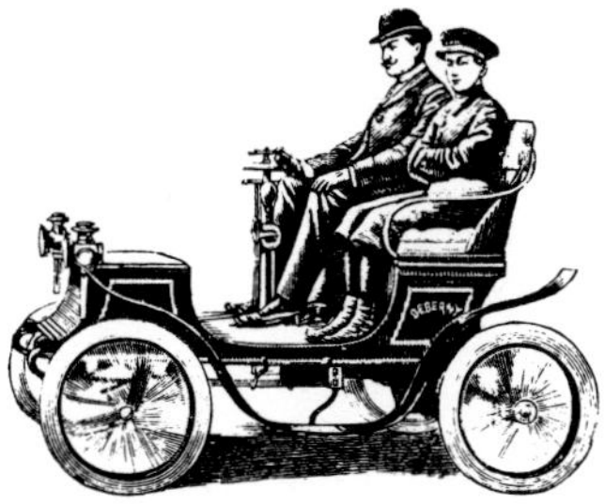

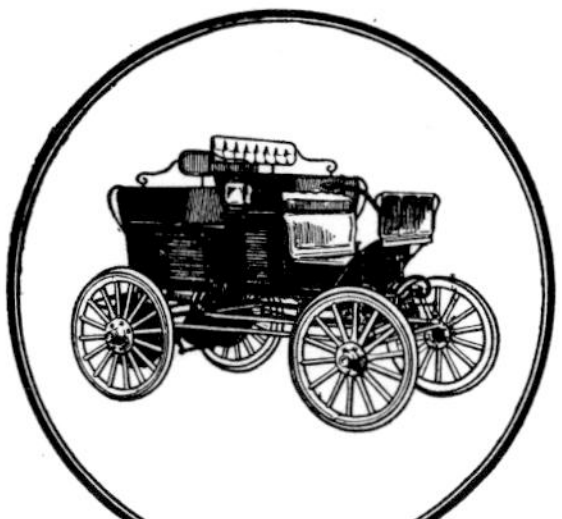

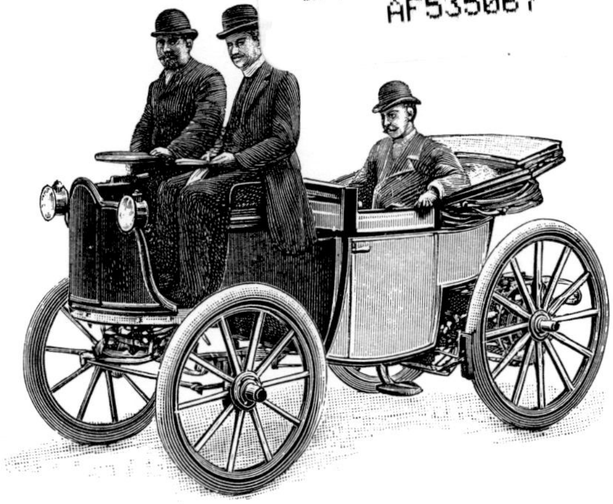

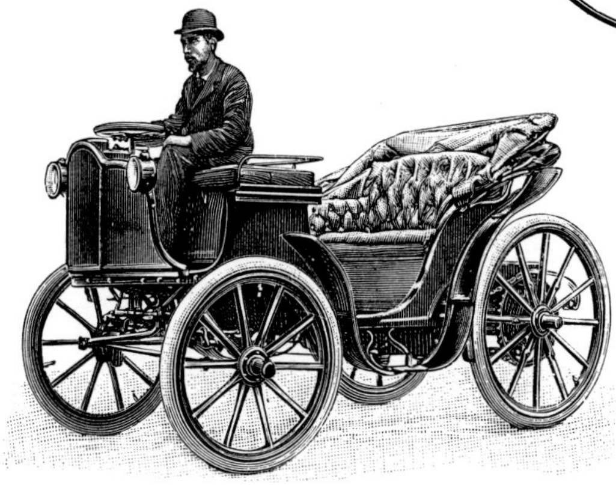

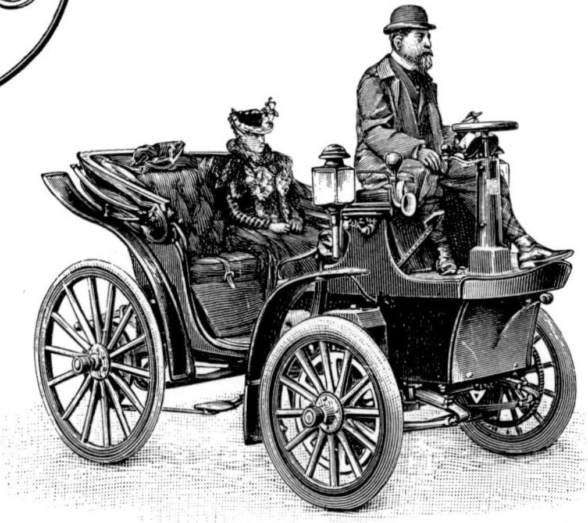

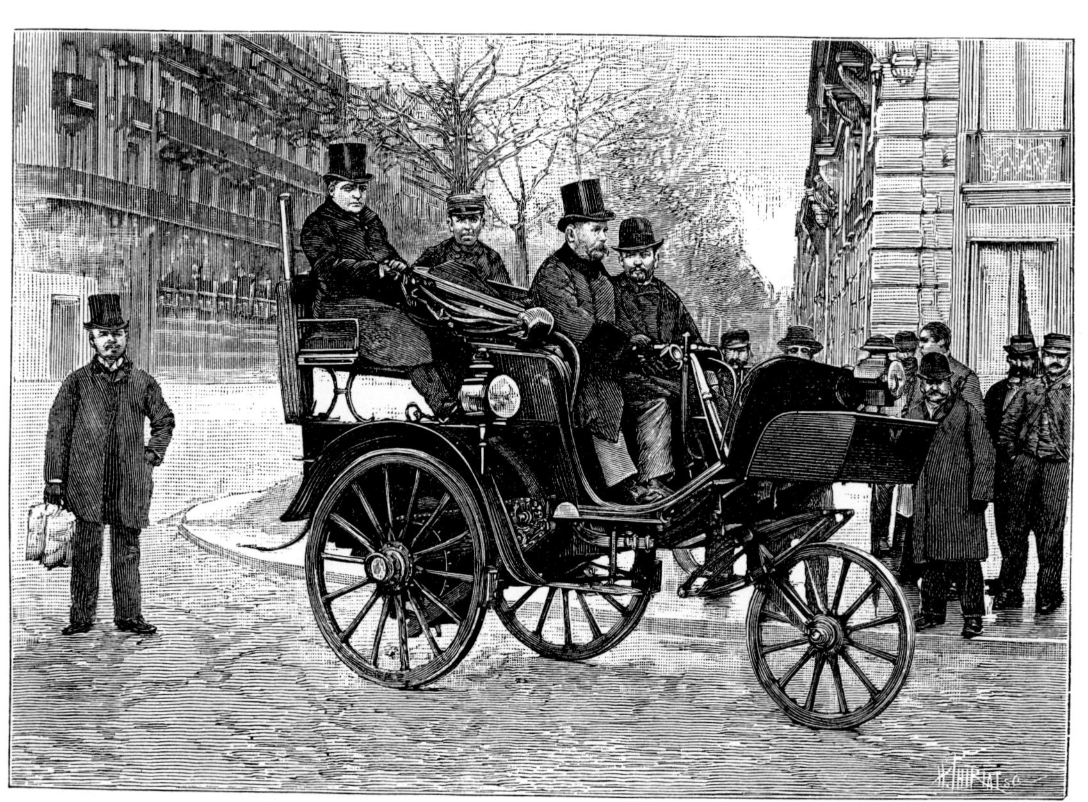

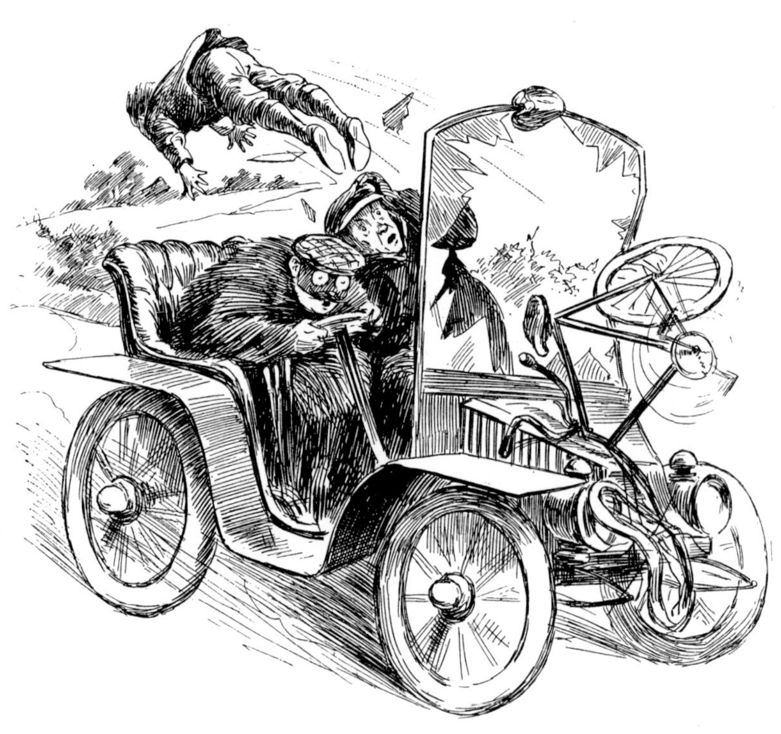

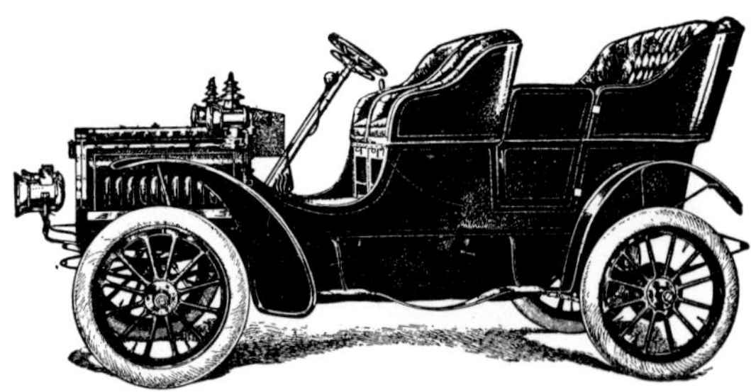

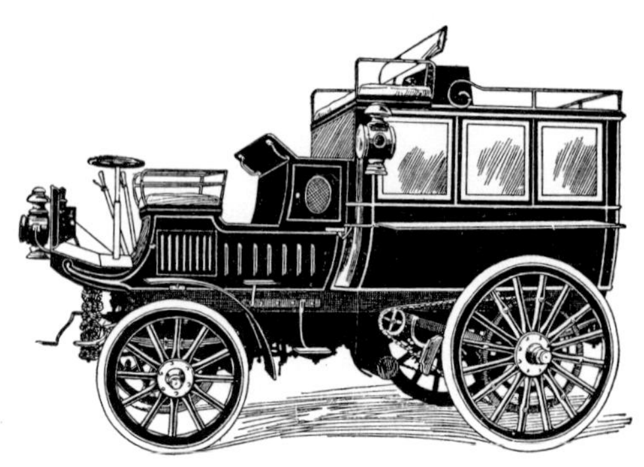

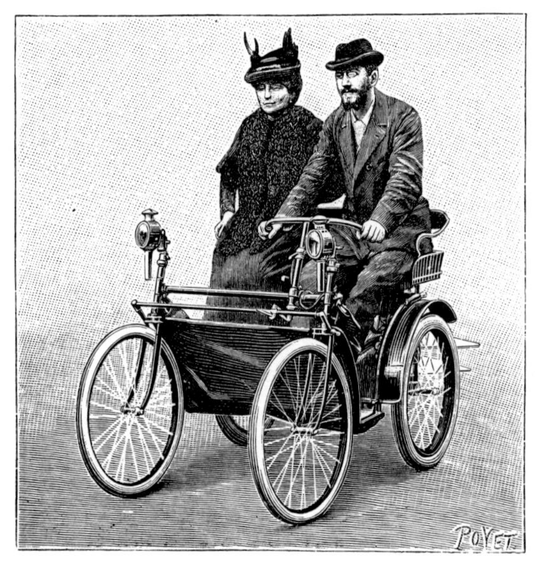
POYET

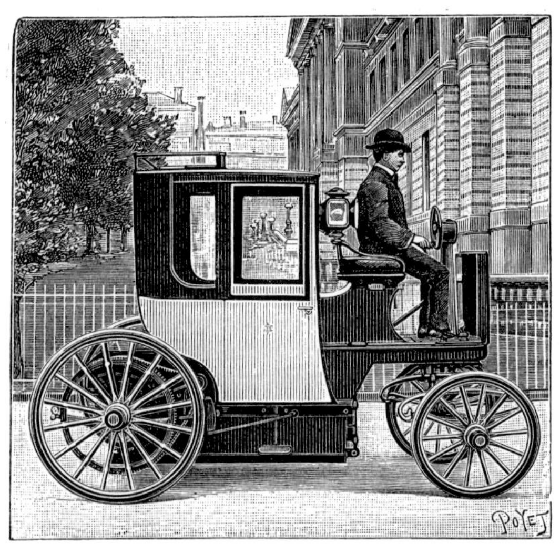
POYET

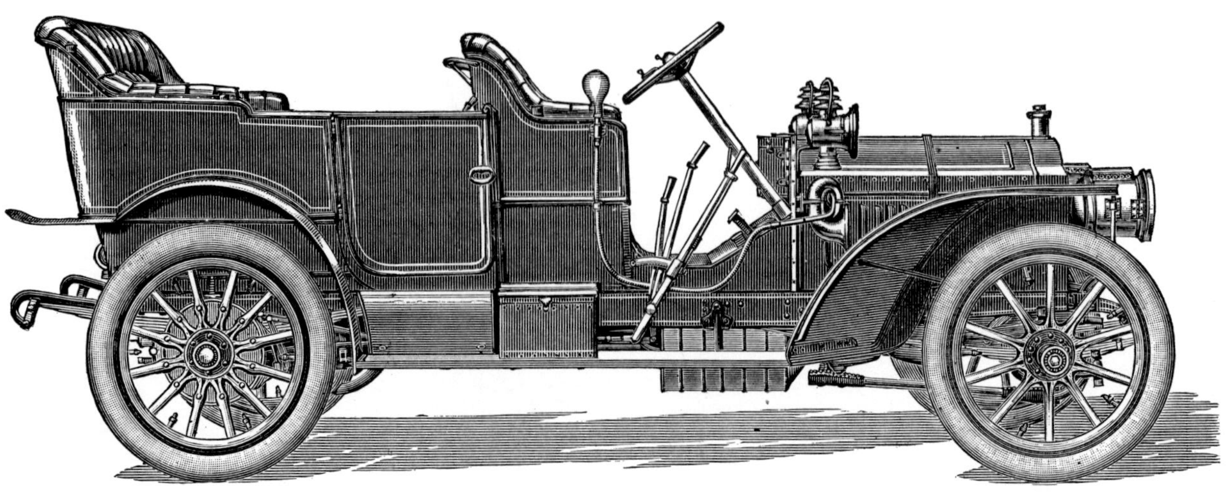

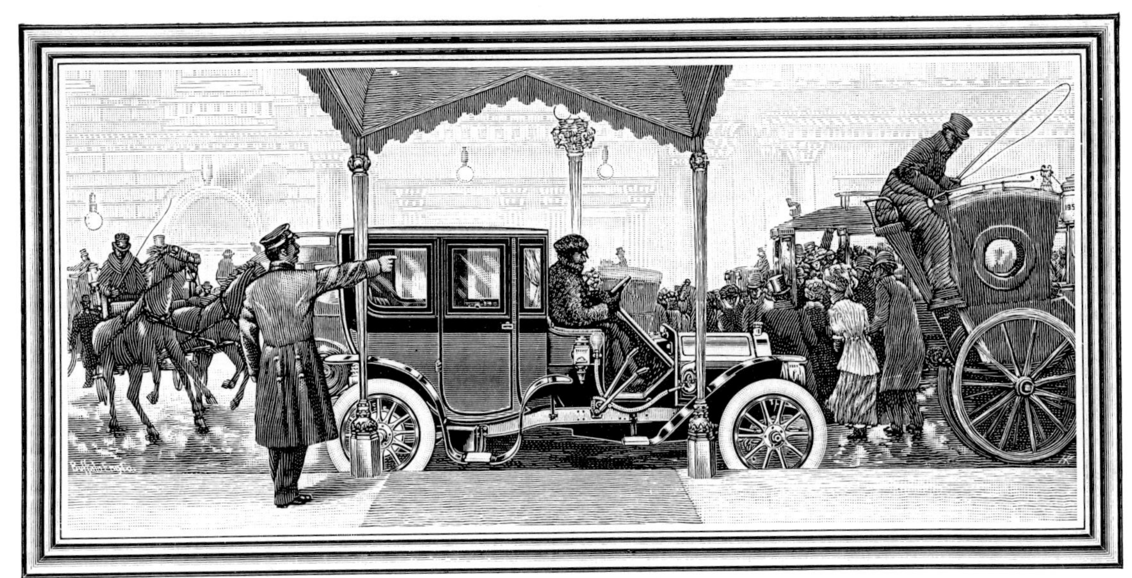

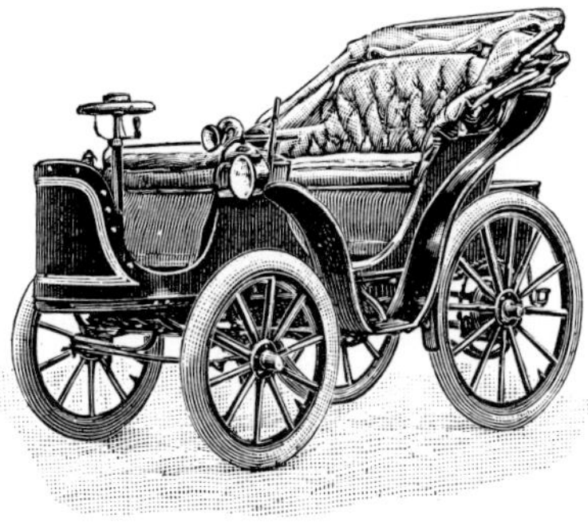

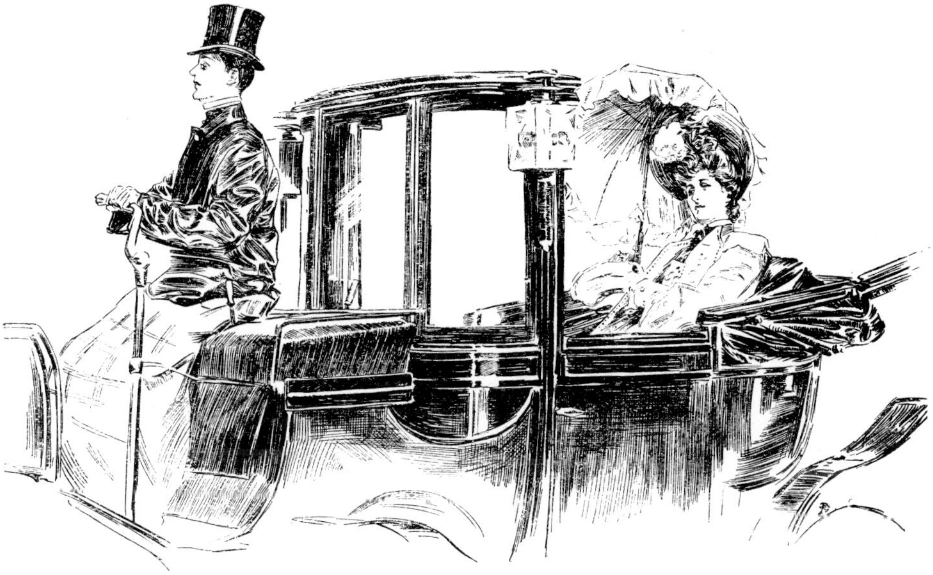

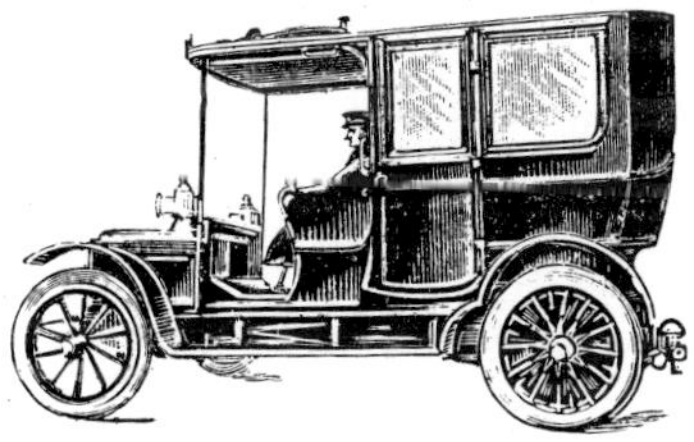

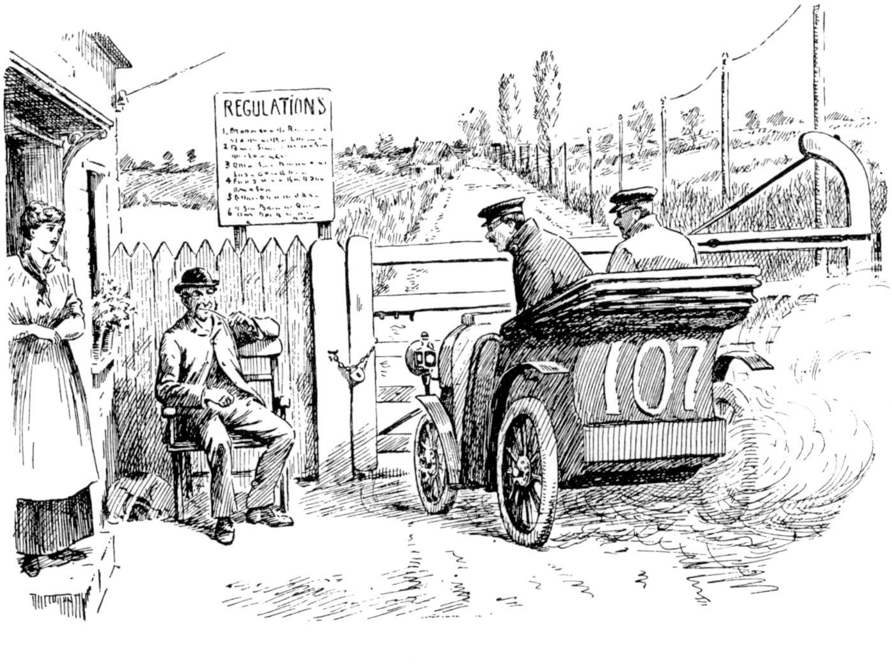

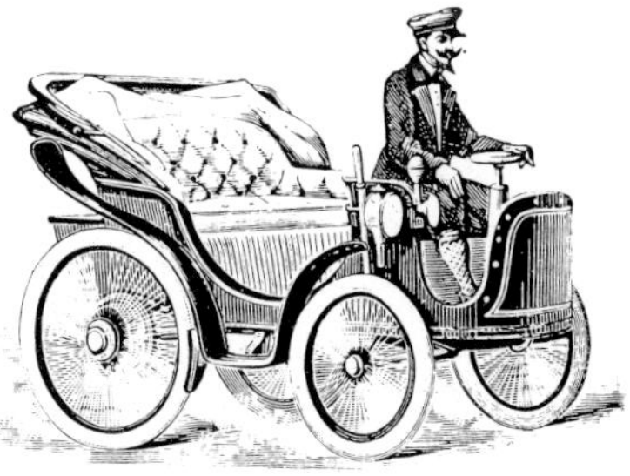

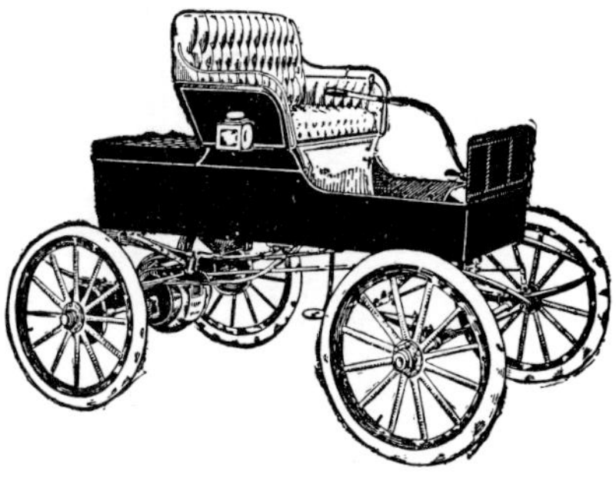

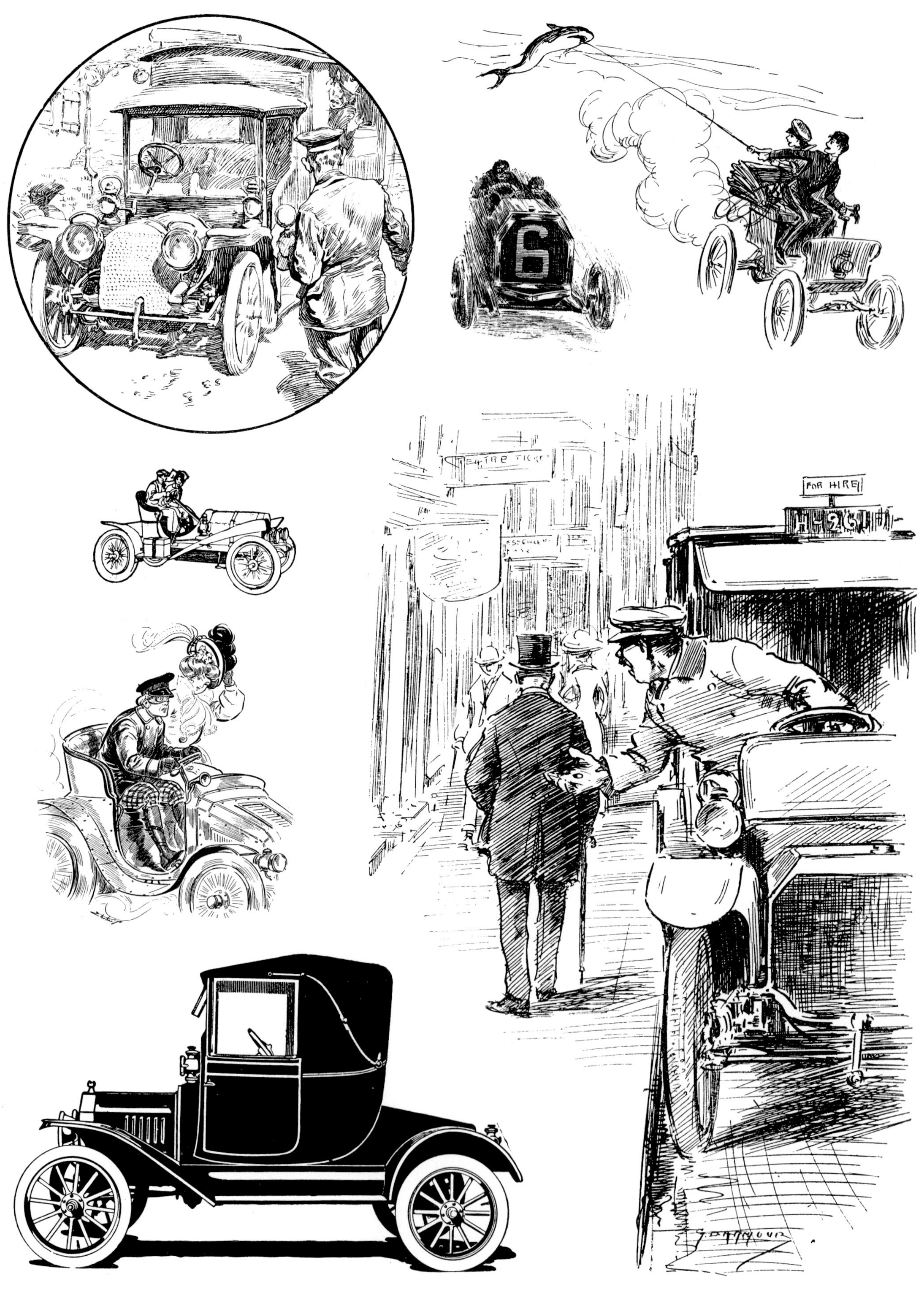
6
FOR HIRE
H-26

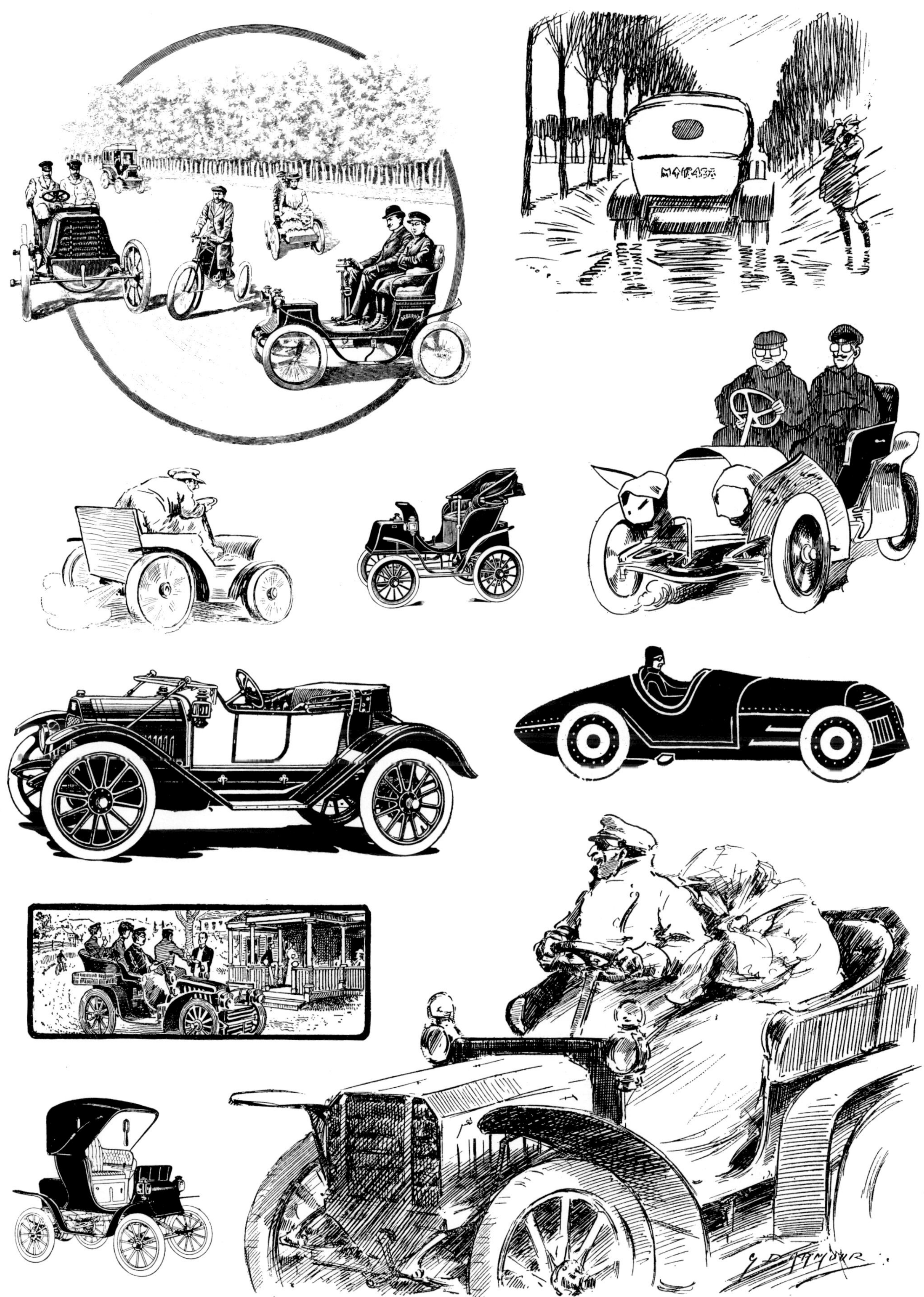

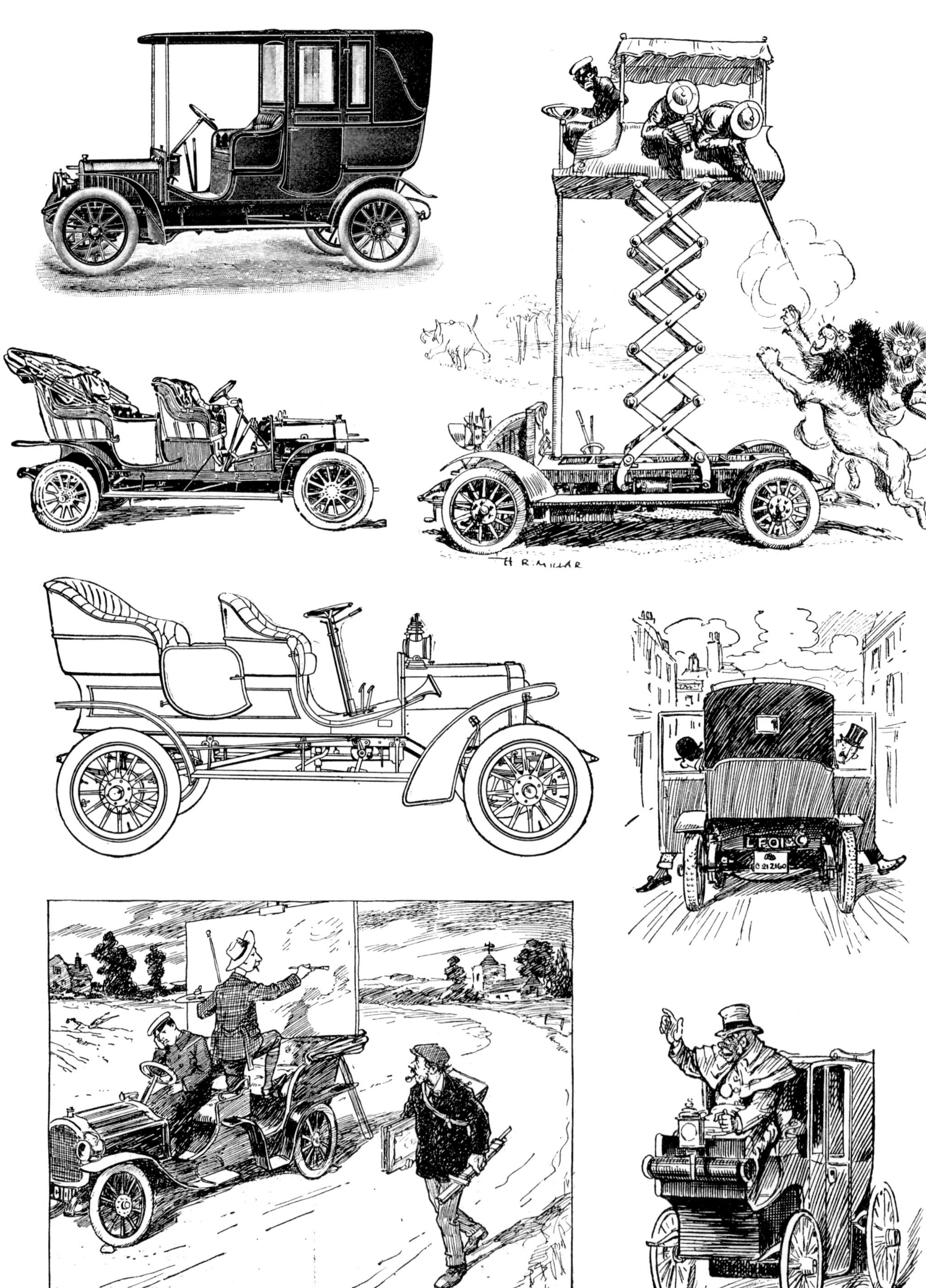
H. R. MILLAR
LEO. MORROW

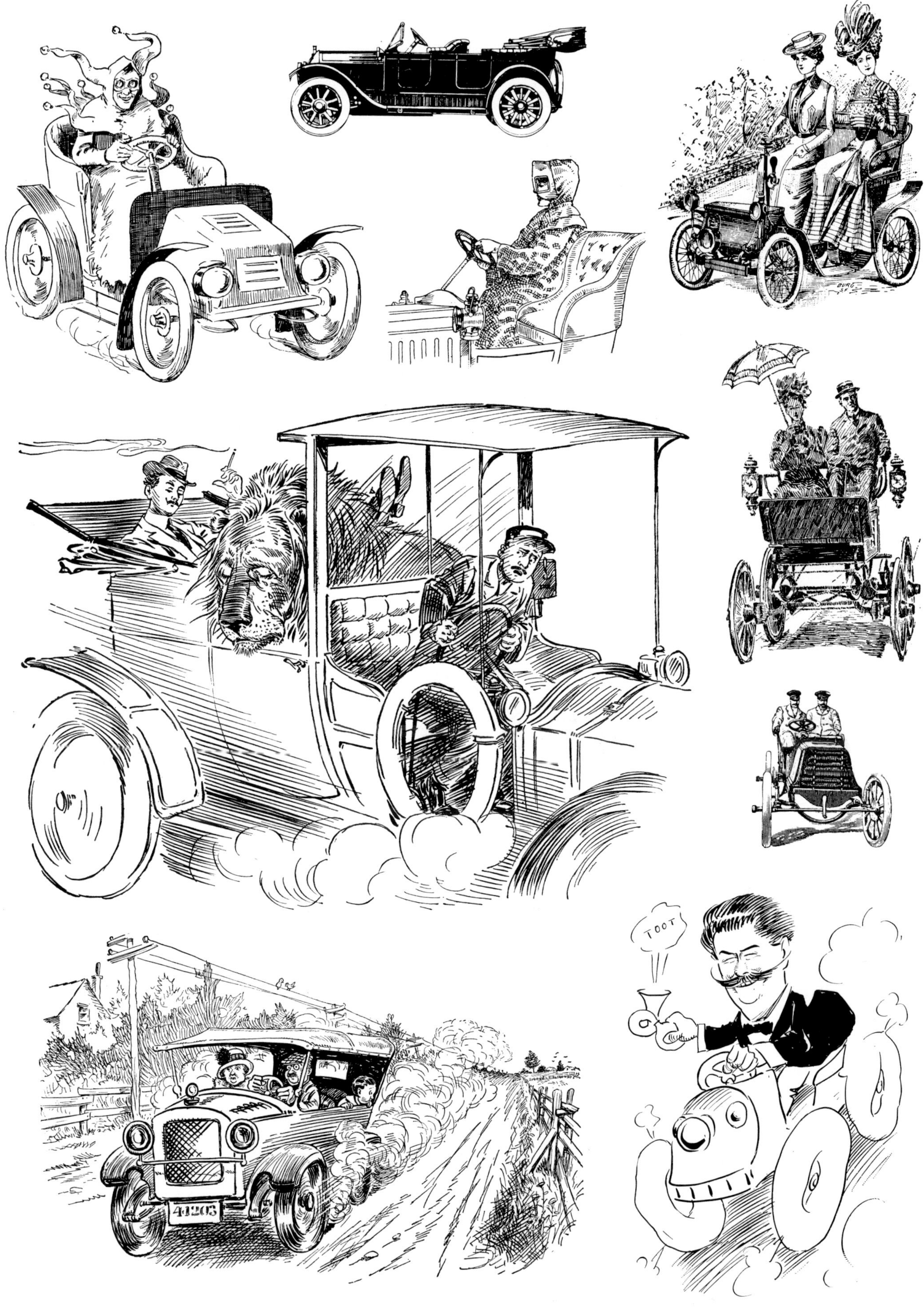
TOOT
44203

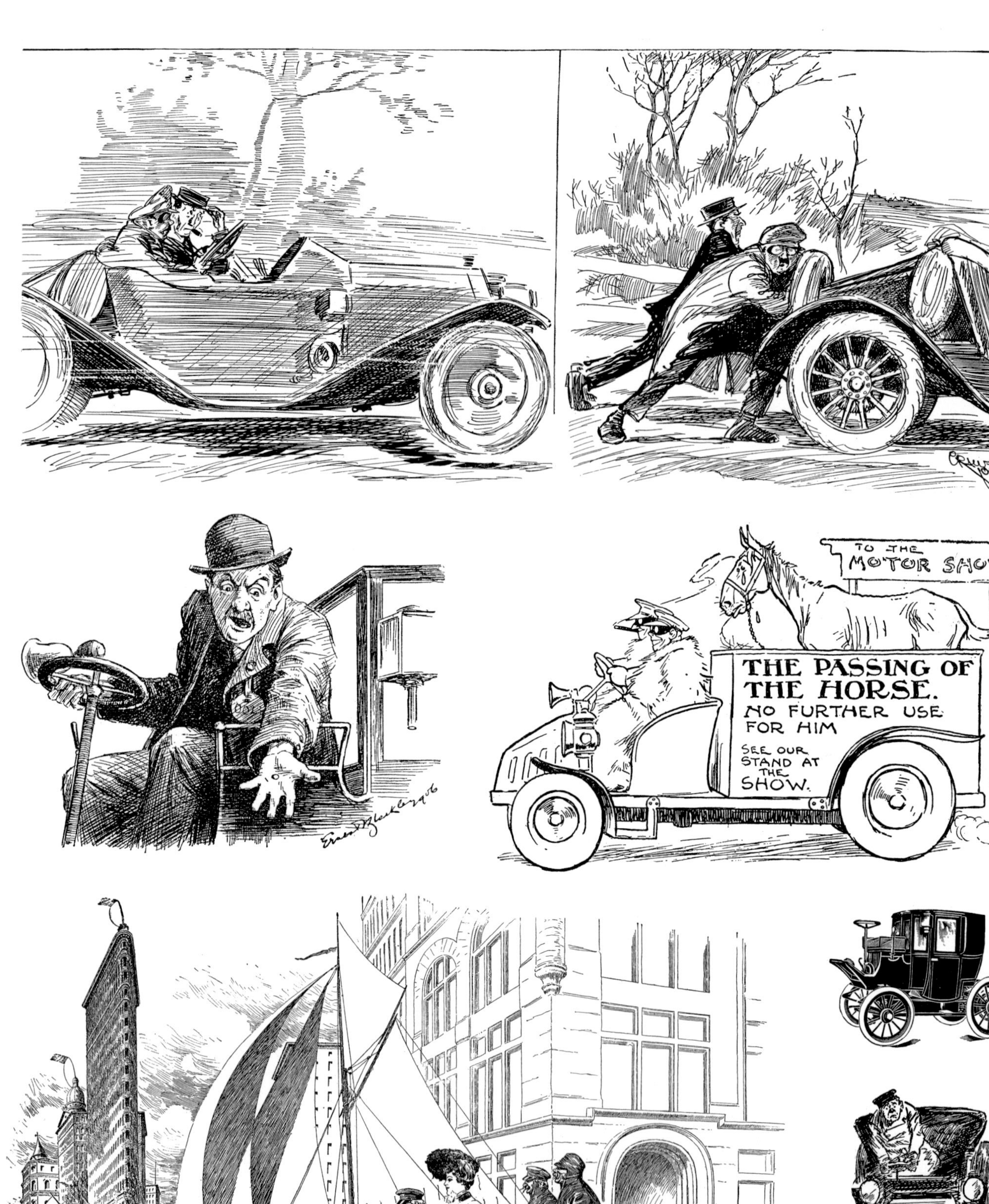
TO THE
MOTOR SHOW
THE PASSING OF
THE HORSE.
NO FURTHER USE
FOR HIM
SEE OUR
STAND AT
THE
SHOW.

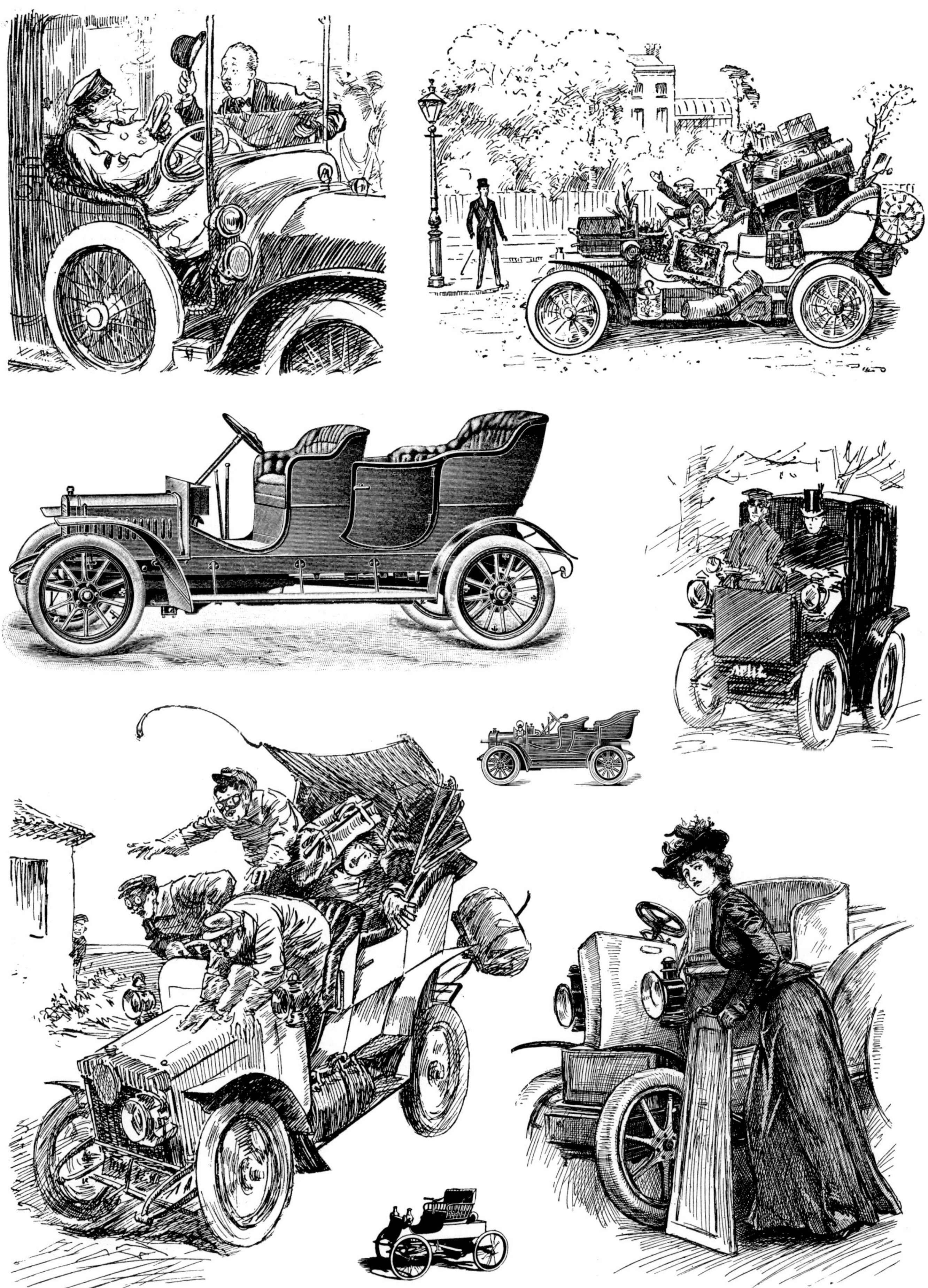

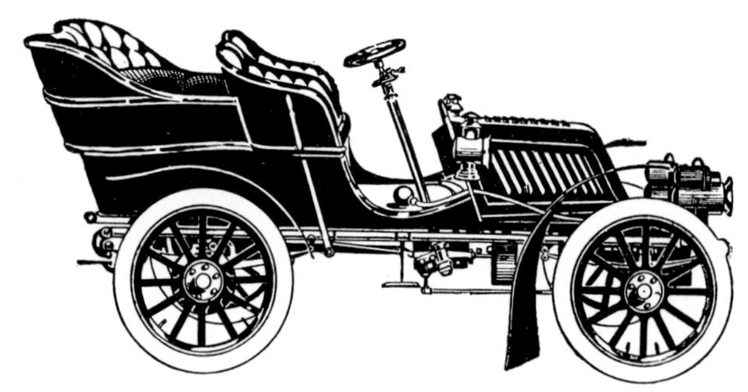

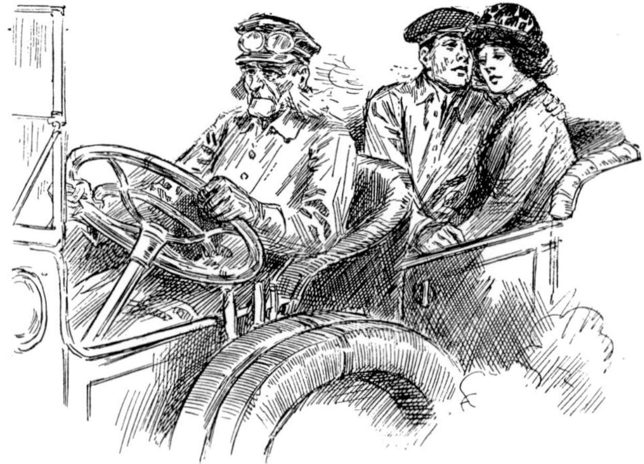

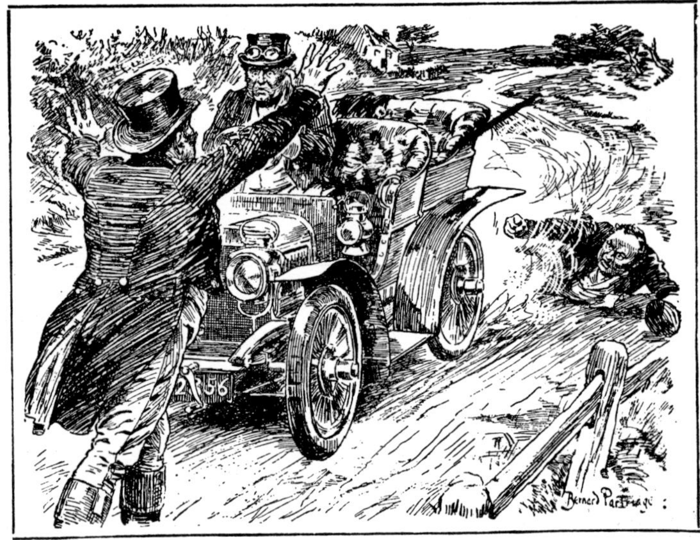
Bernard Partridge

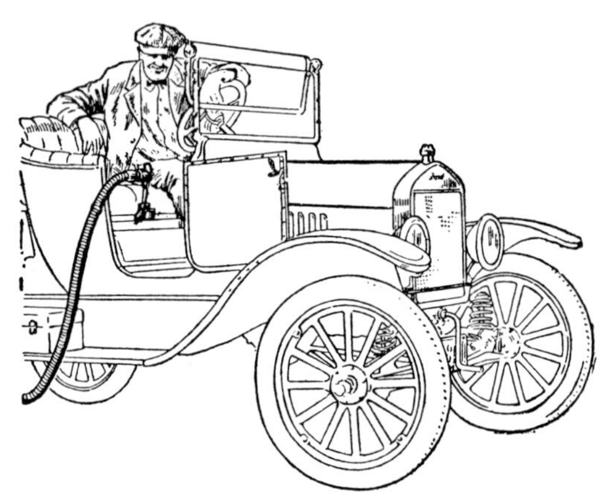

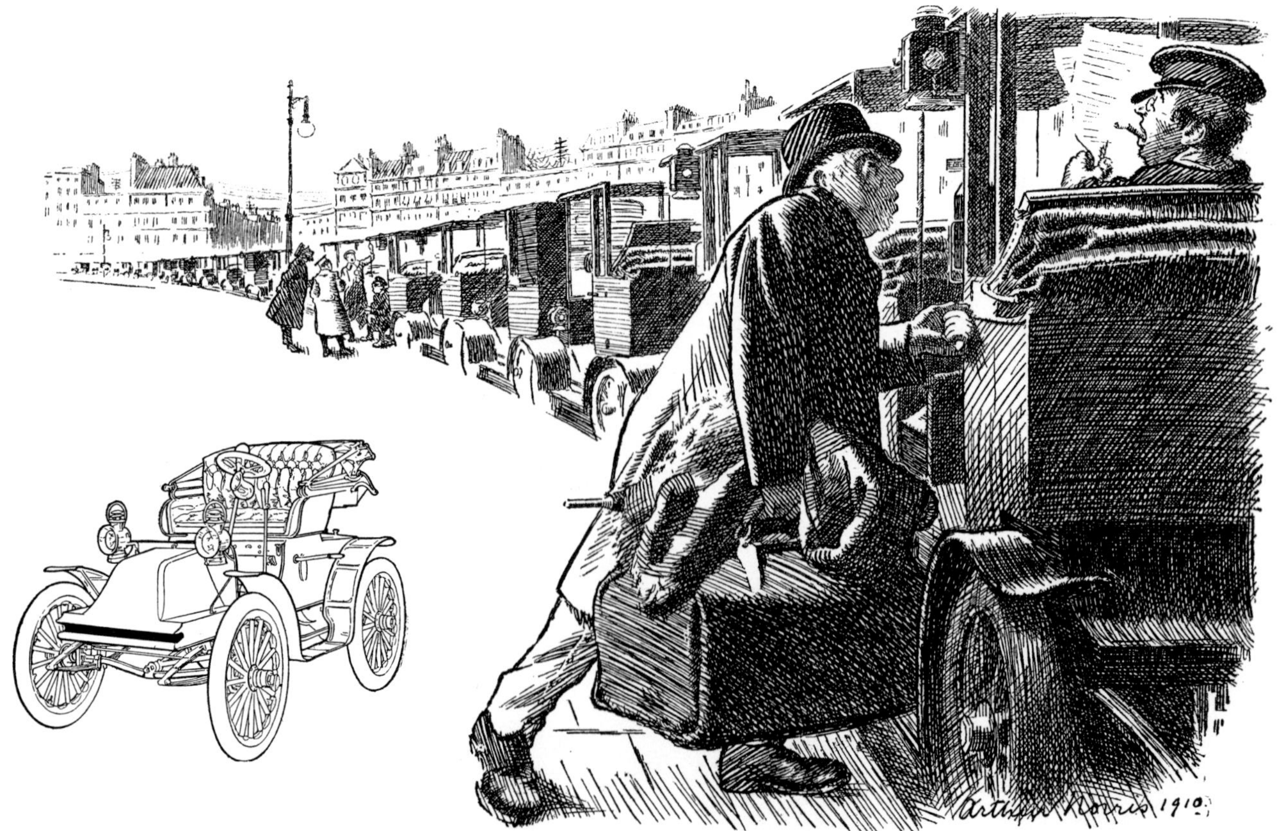

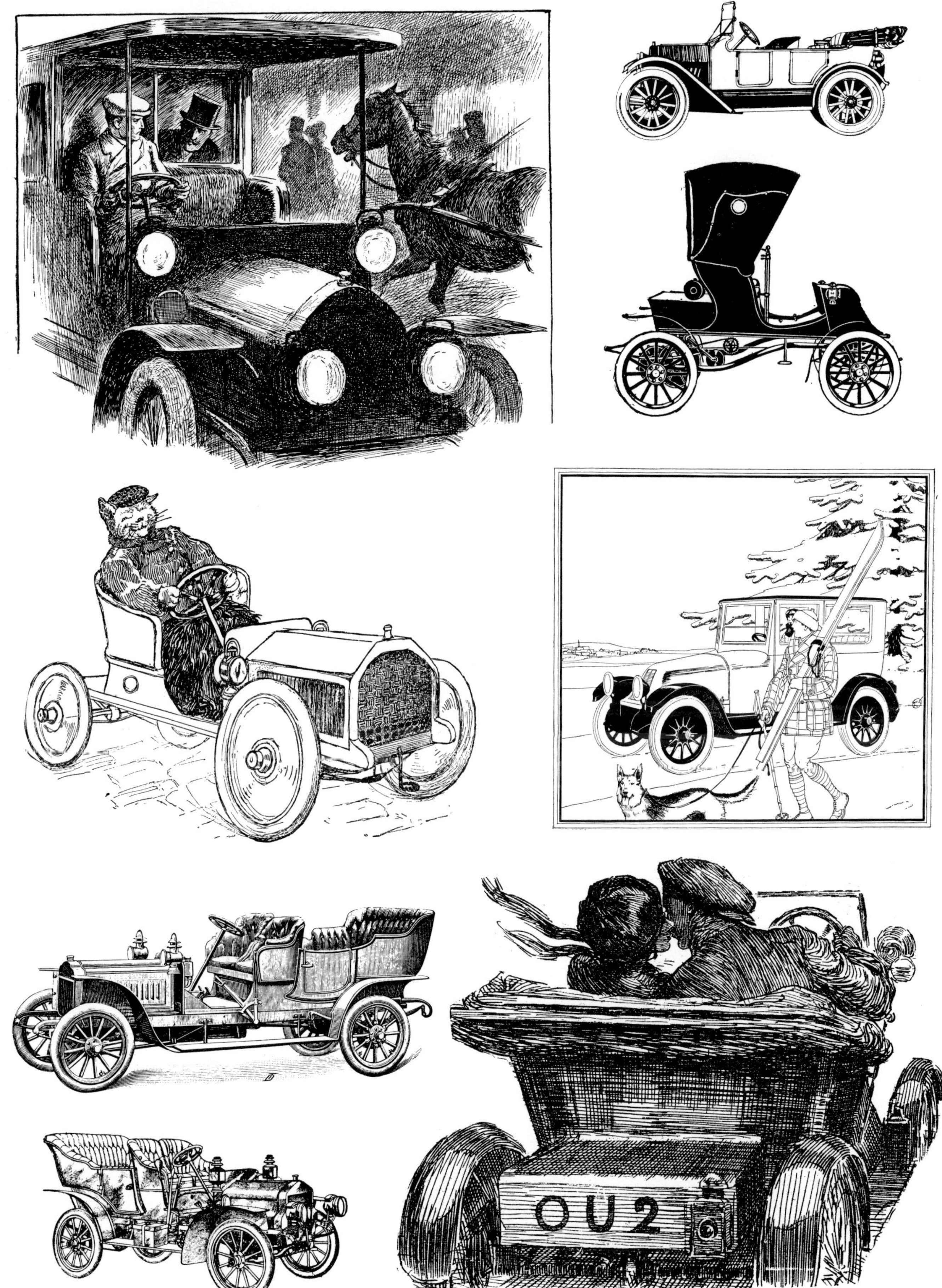
OU2

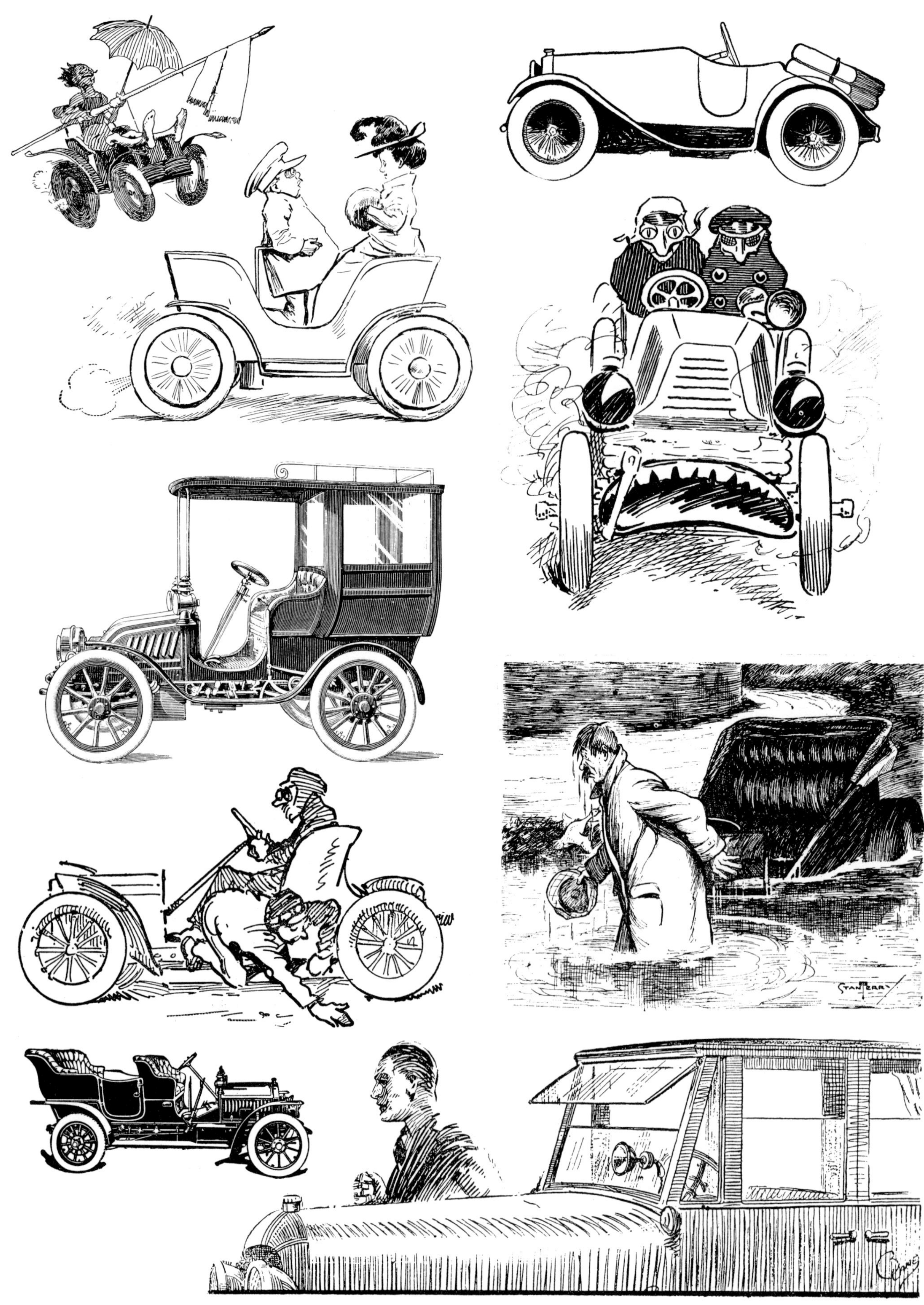
STAN TERRY

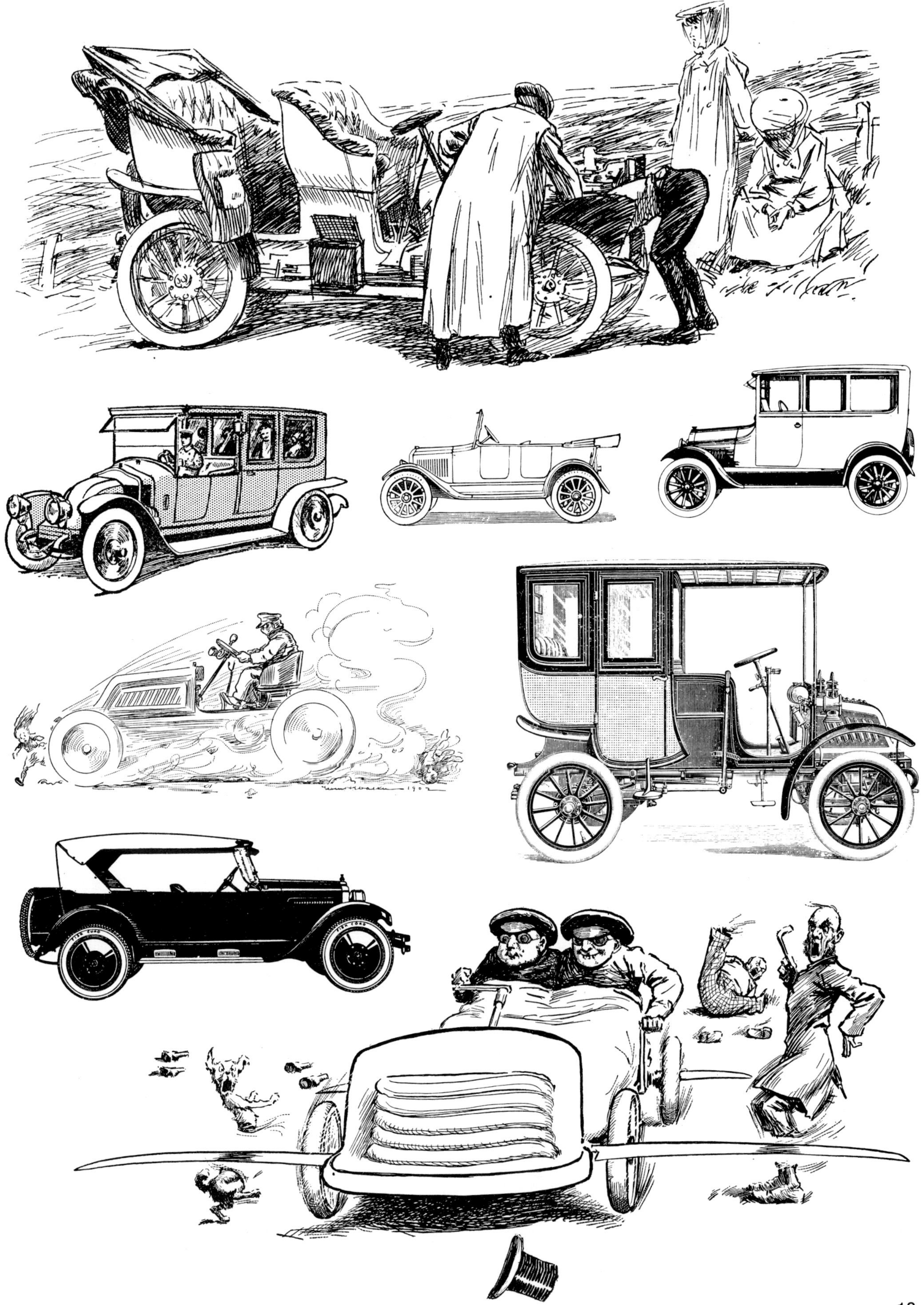

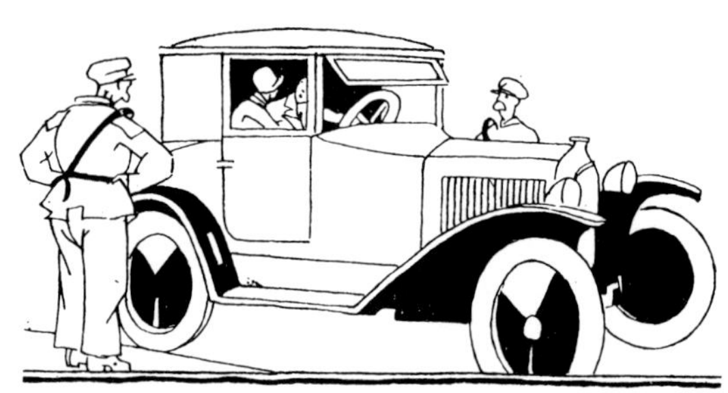
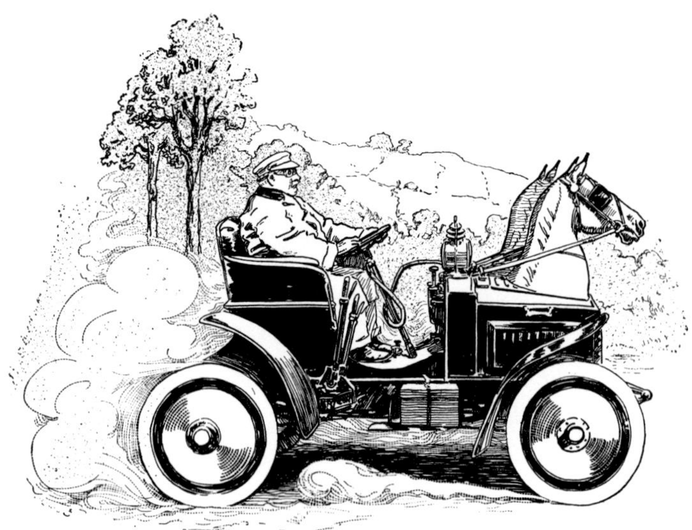
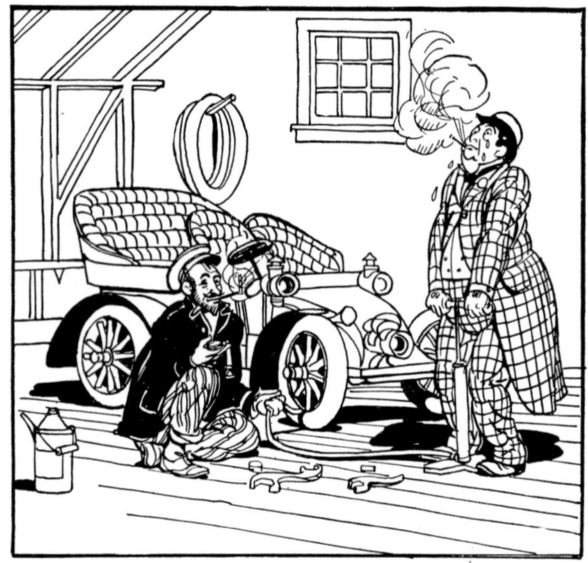
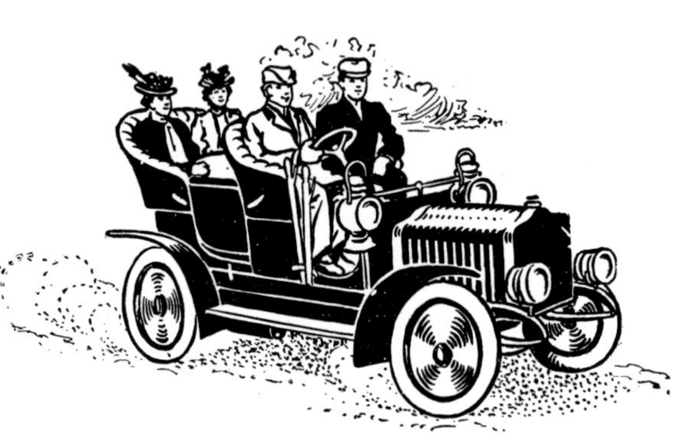
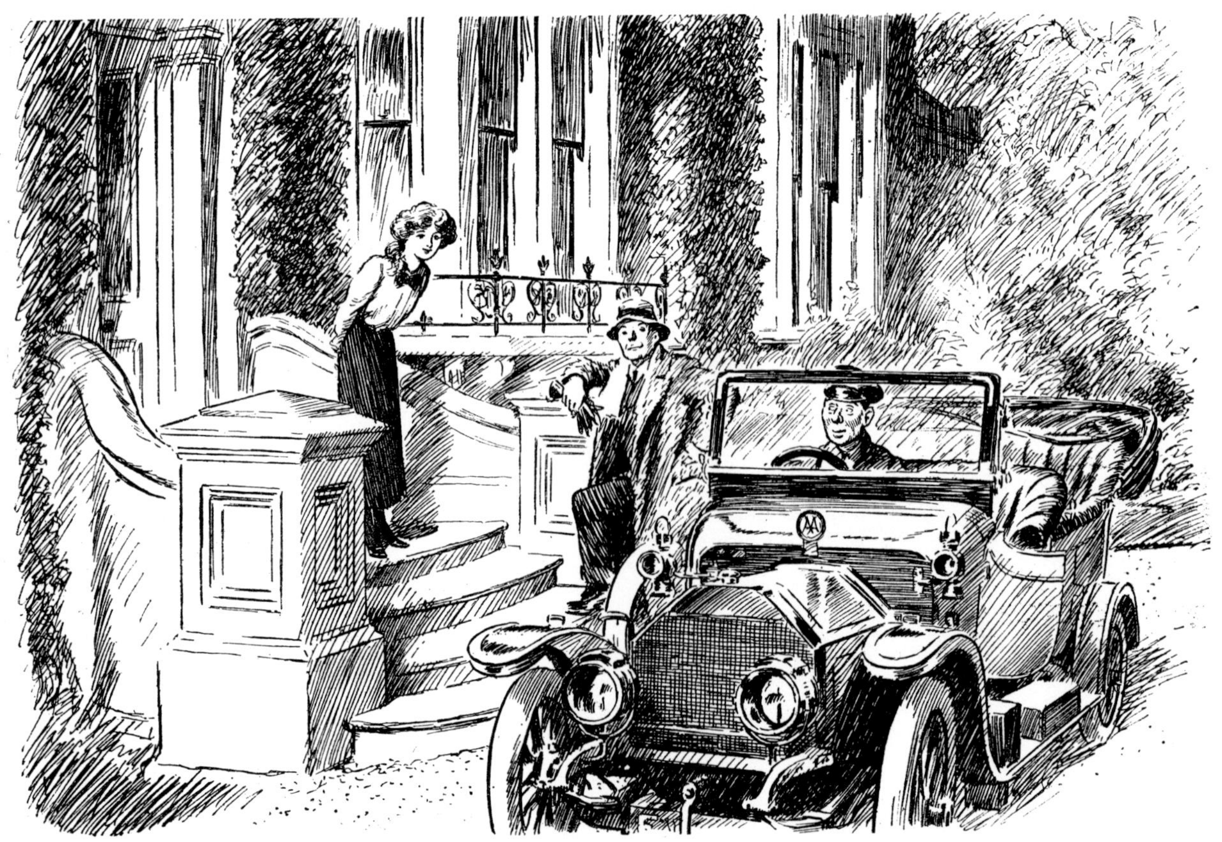

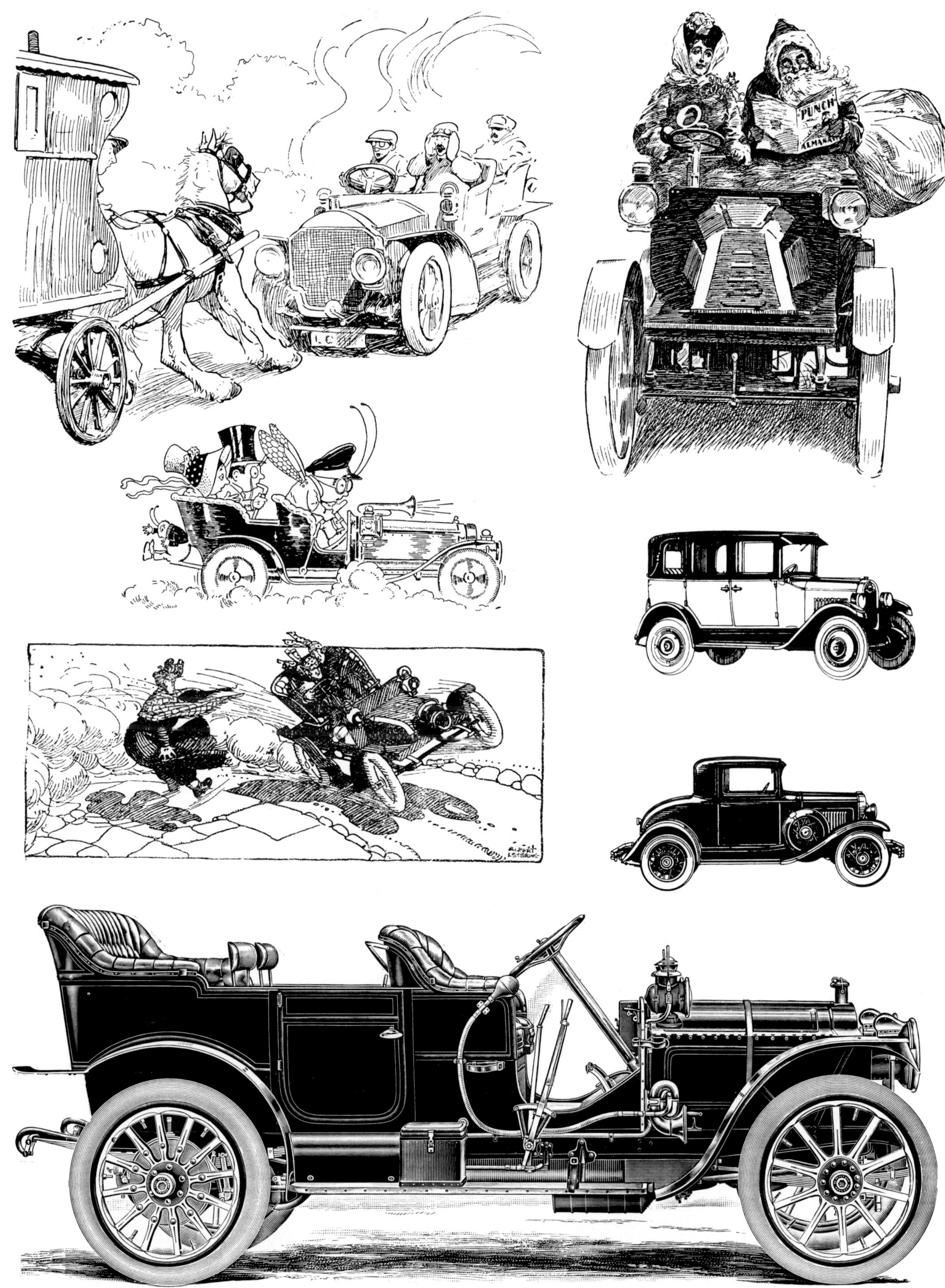
PUNCH

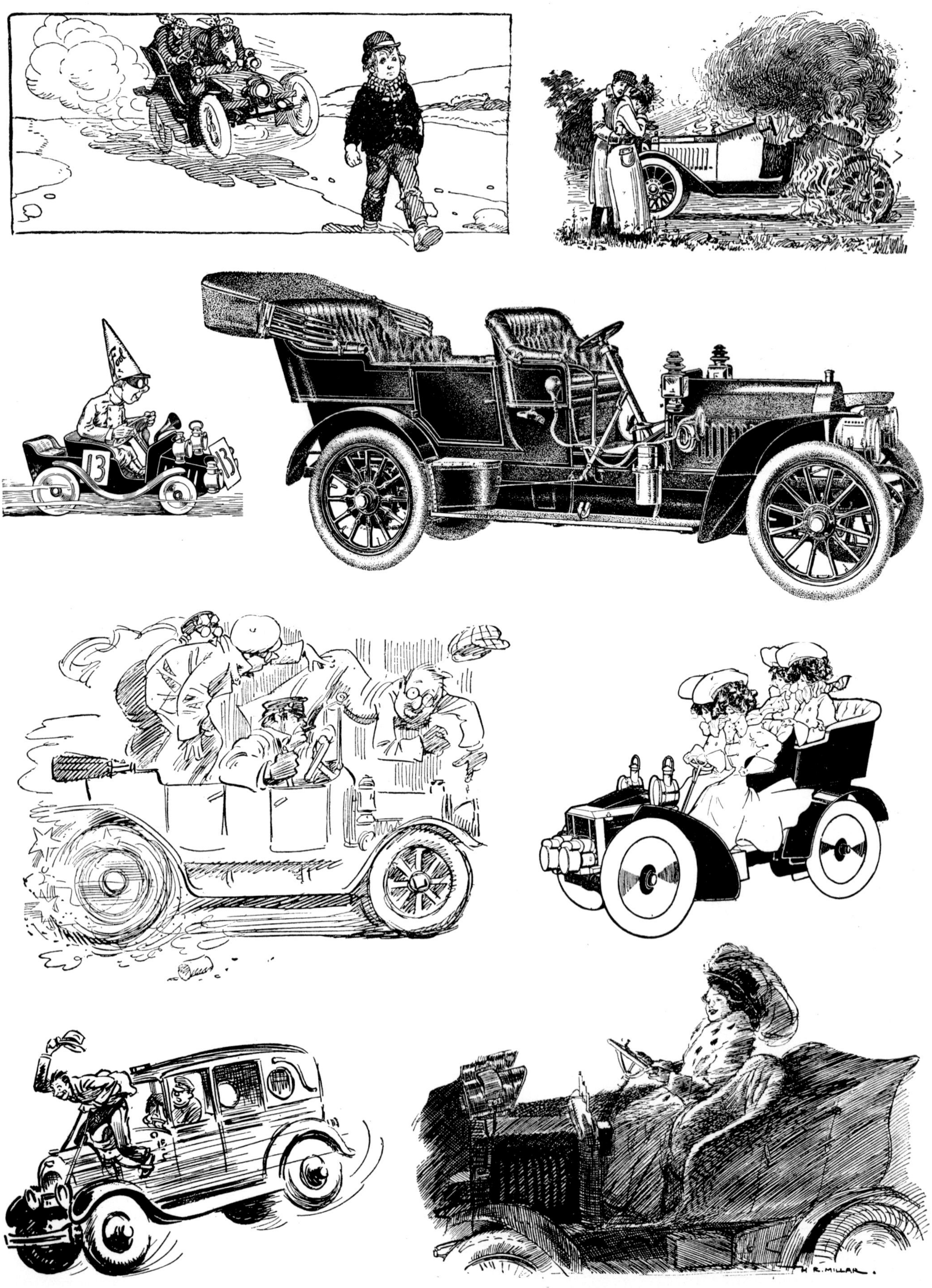
13
13
H. R. MILLAR.

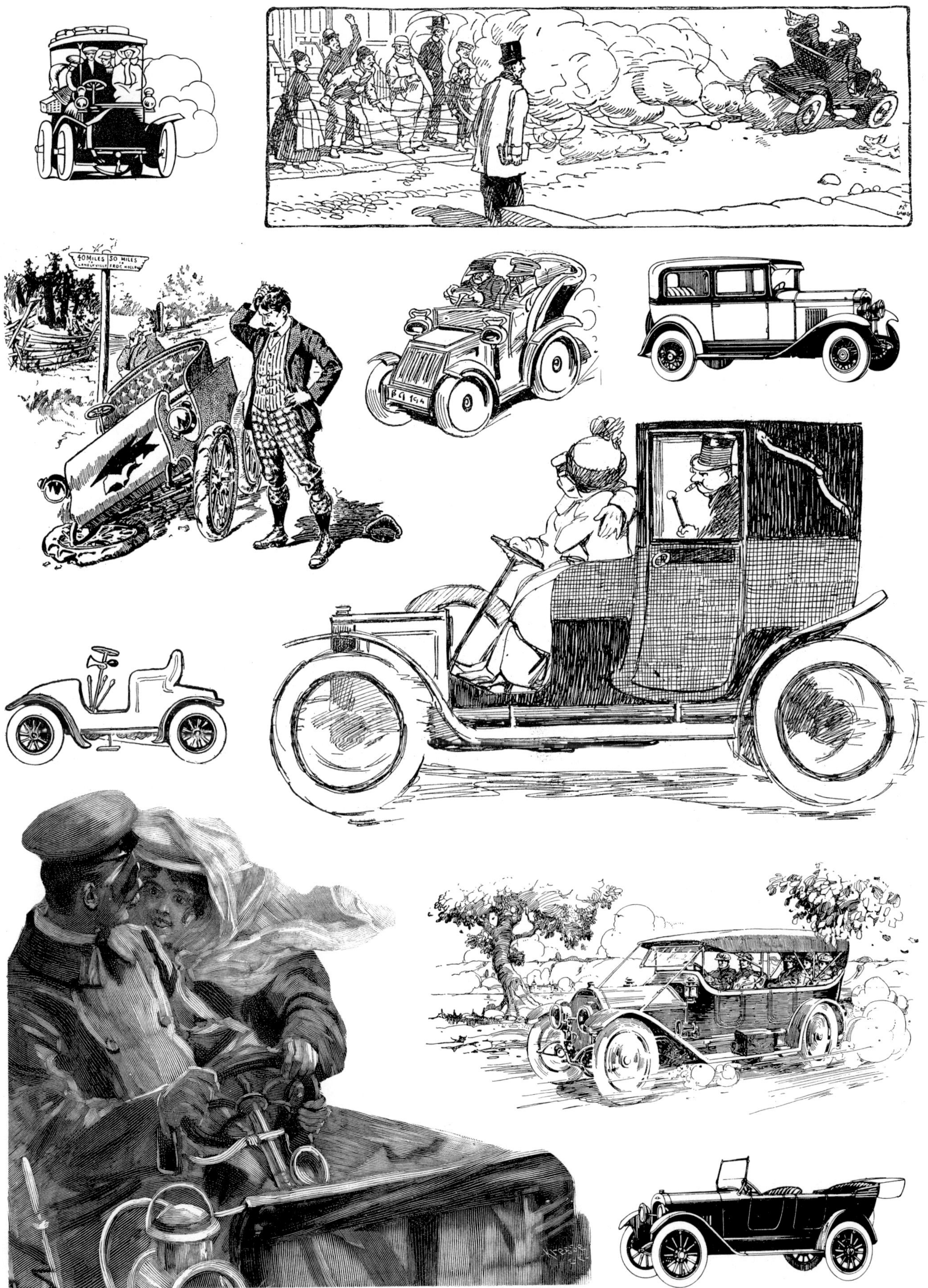
40 MILES
50 MILES

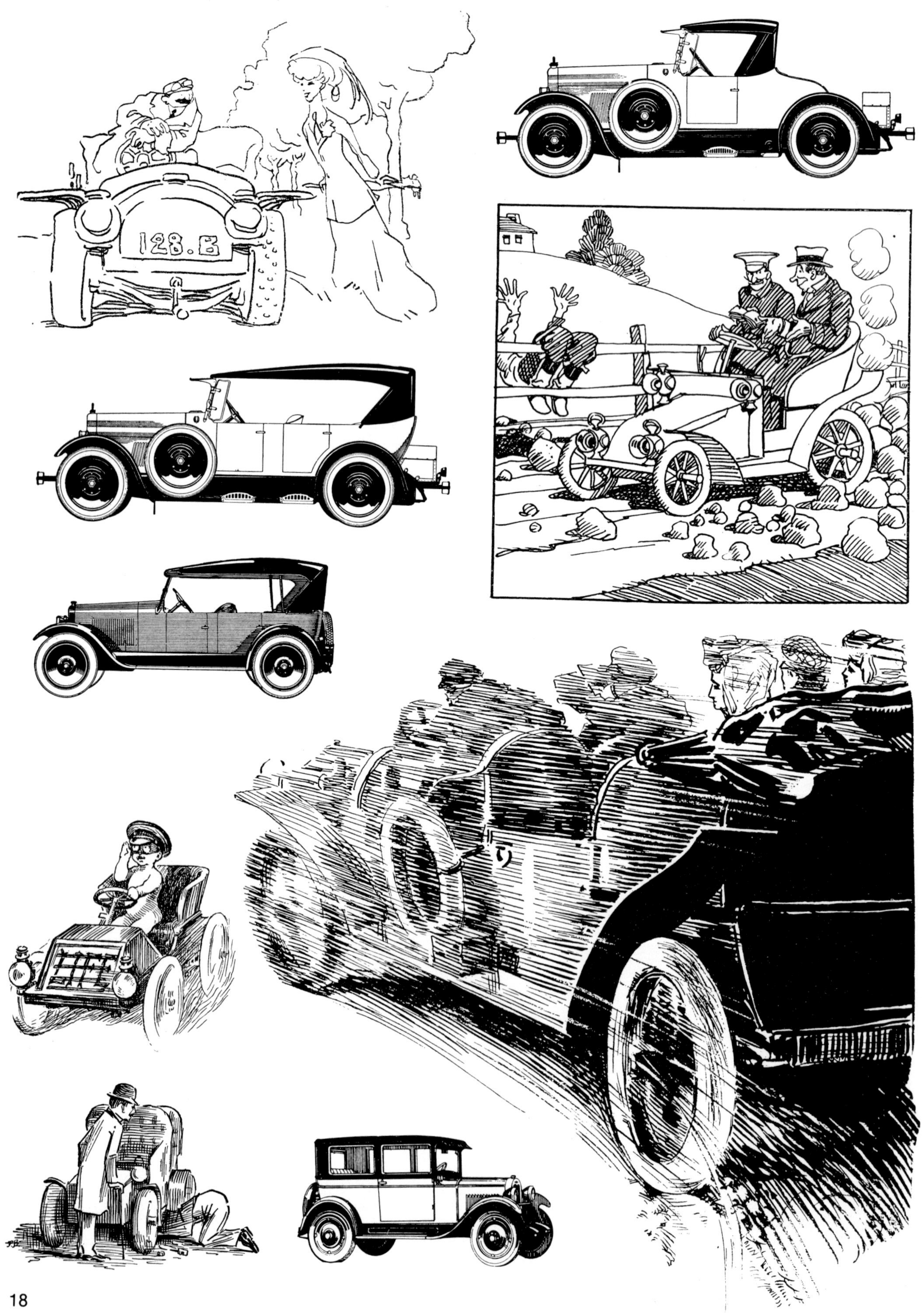
128.B

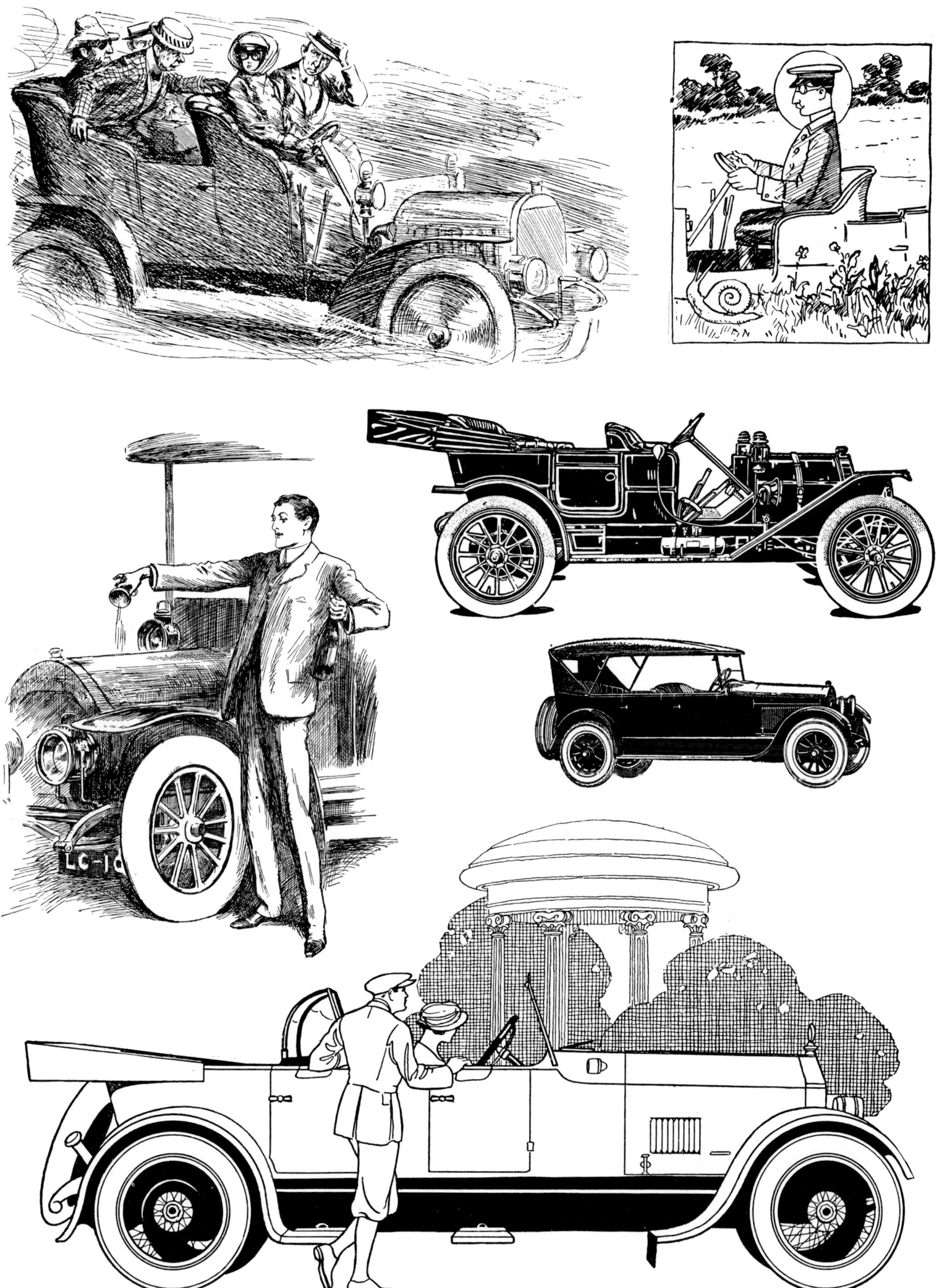

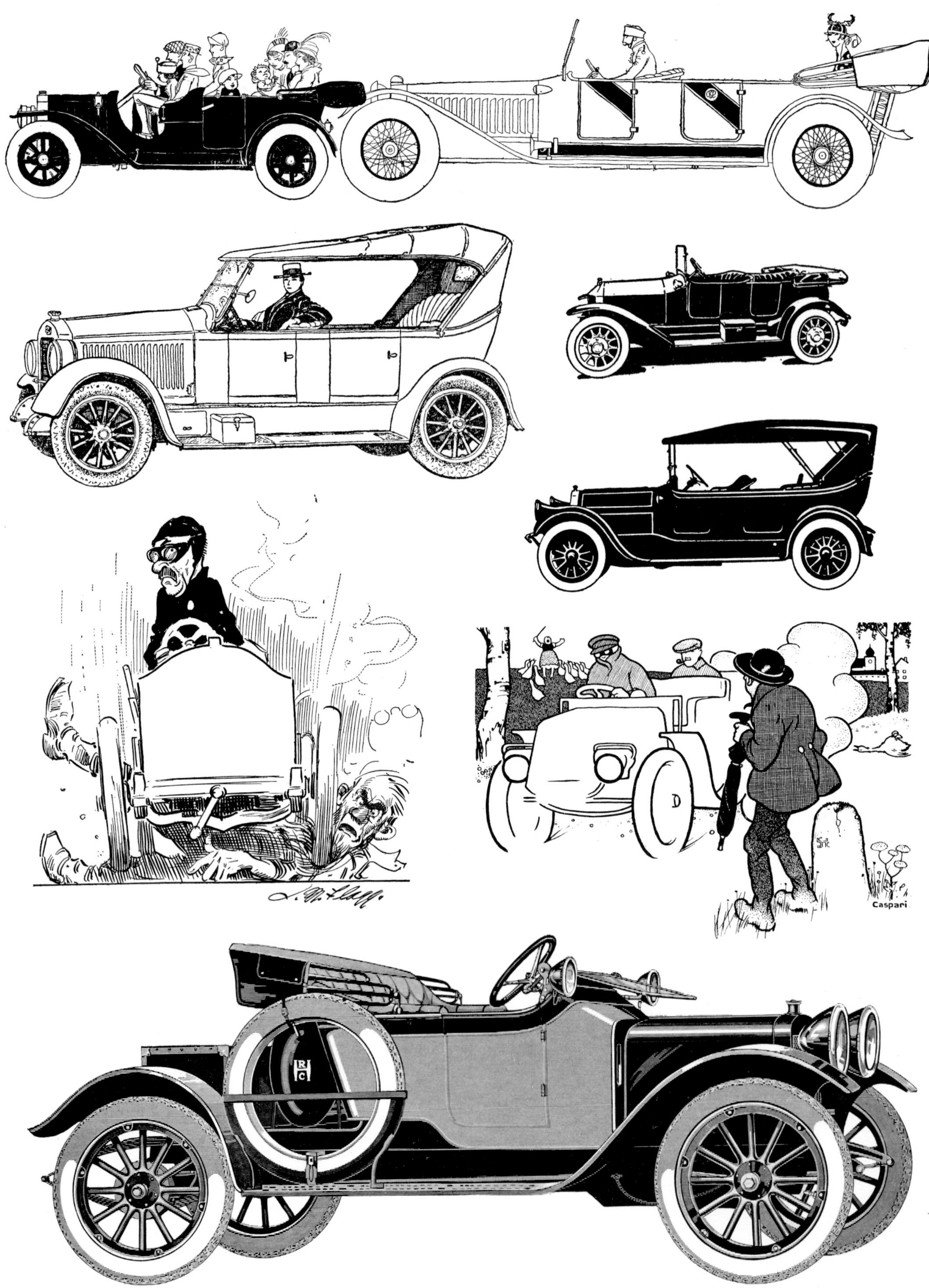
Caspari

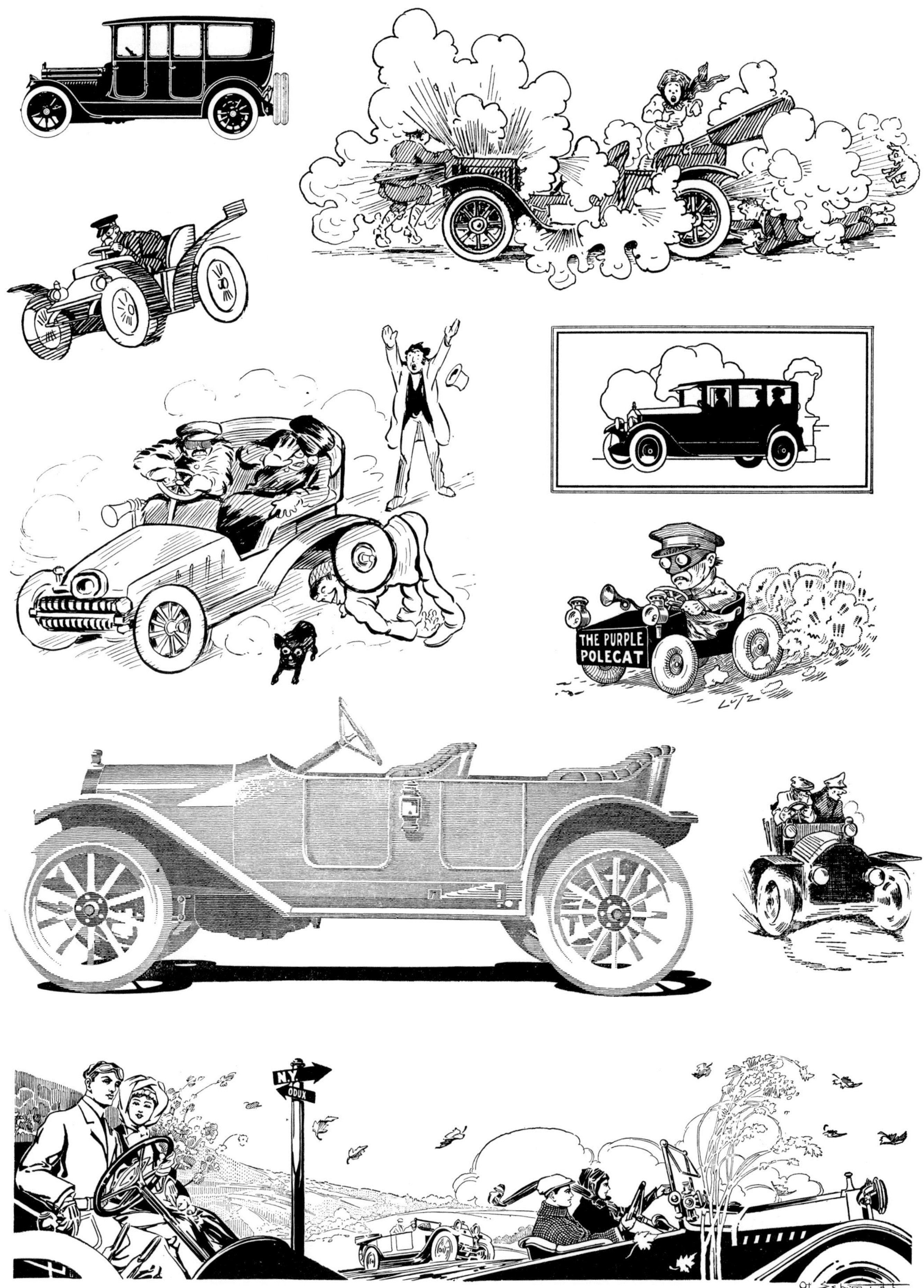
THE PURPLE
POLECAT
N.Y.
ODUX

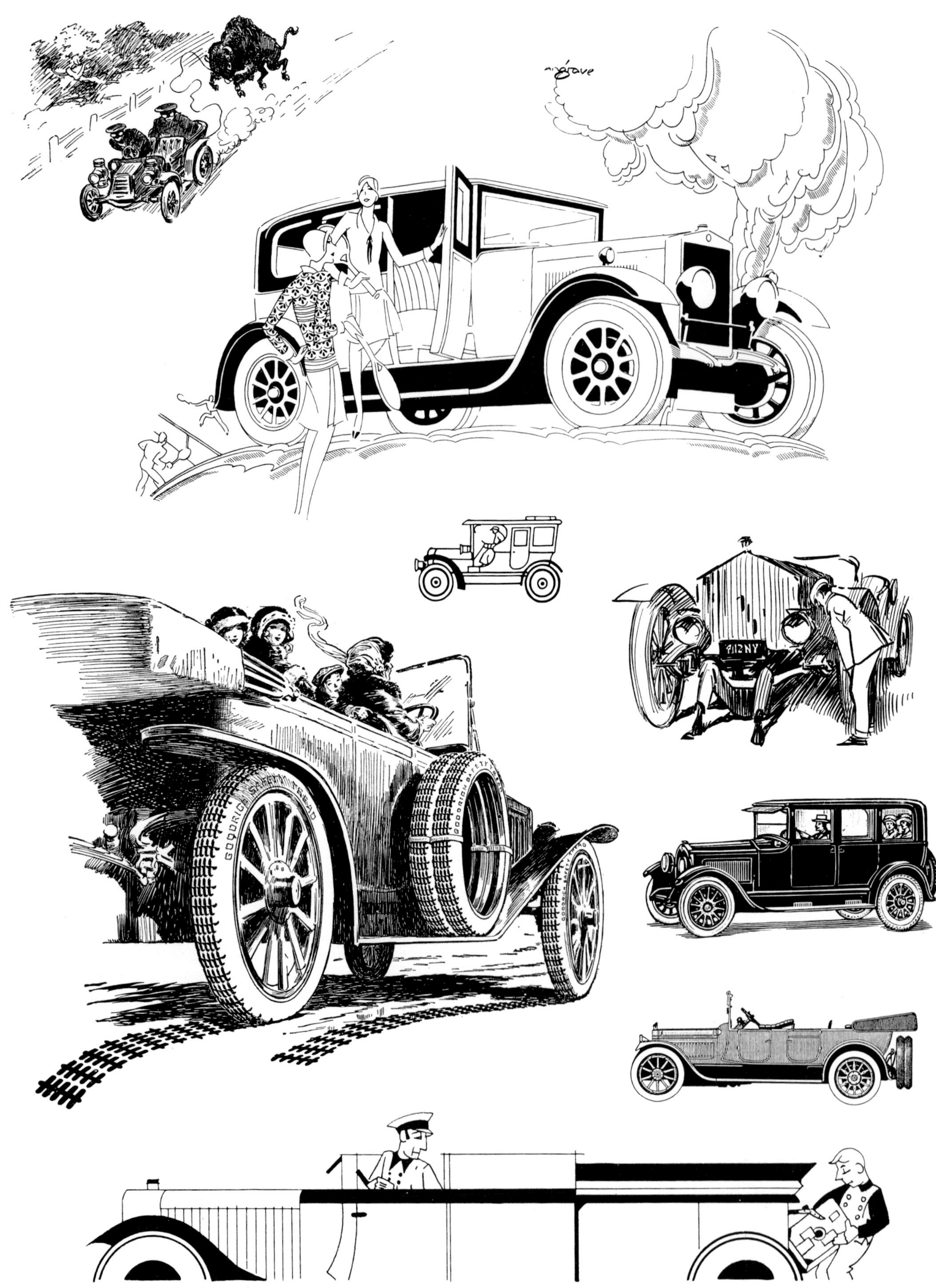
GOODRICH SAFETY TREAD

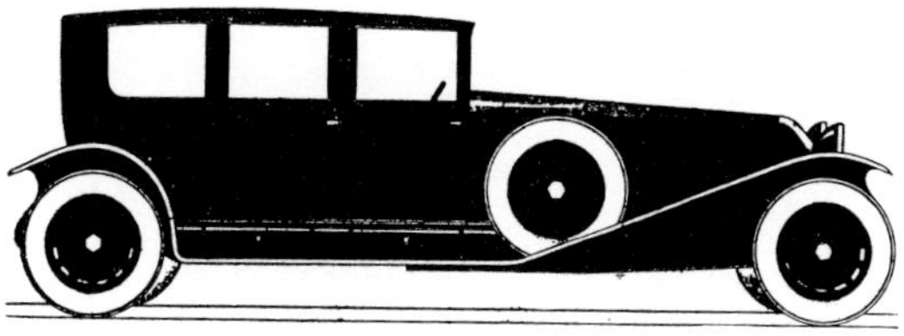

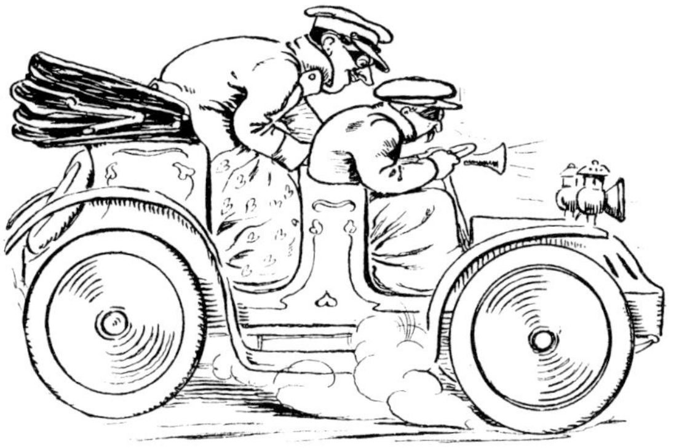

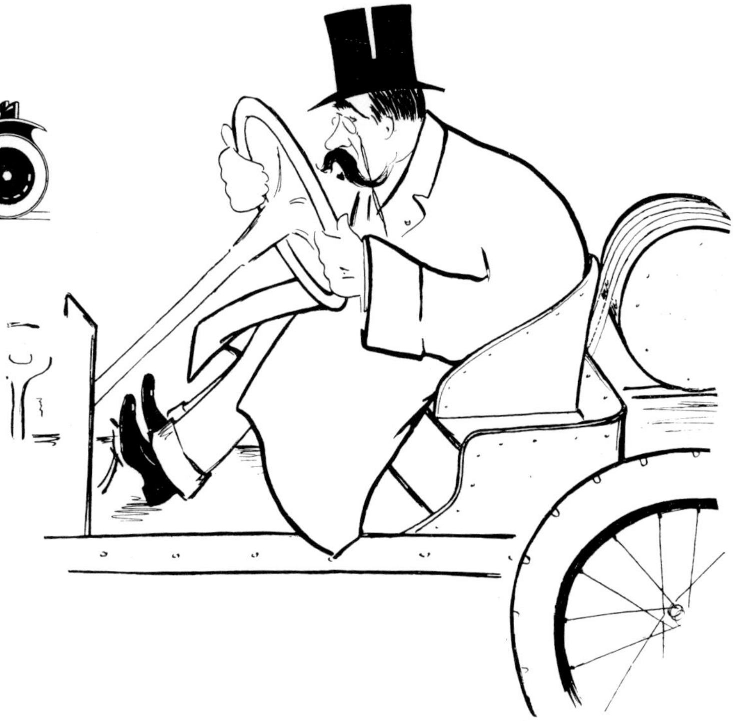

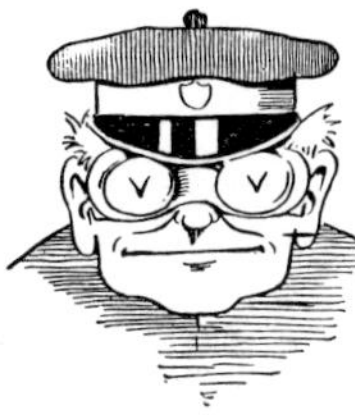

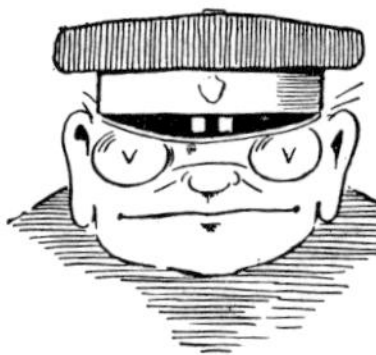

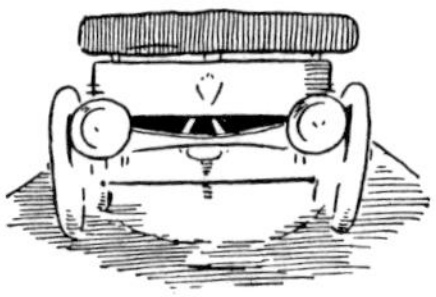

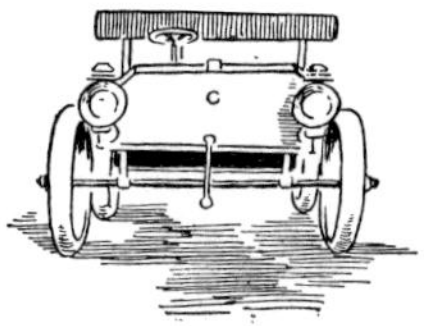

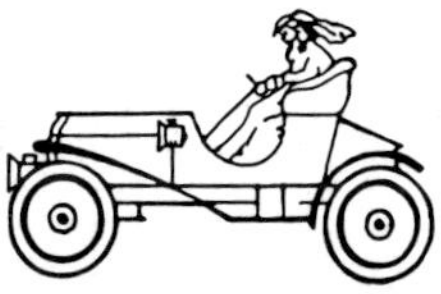

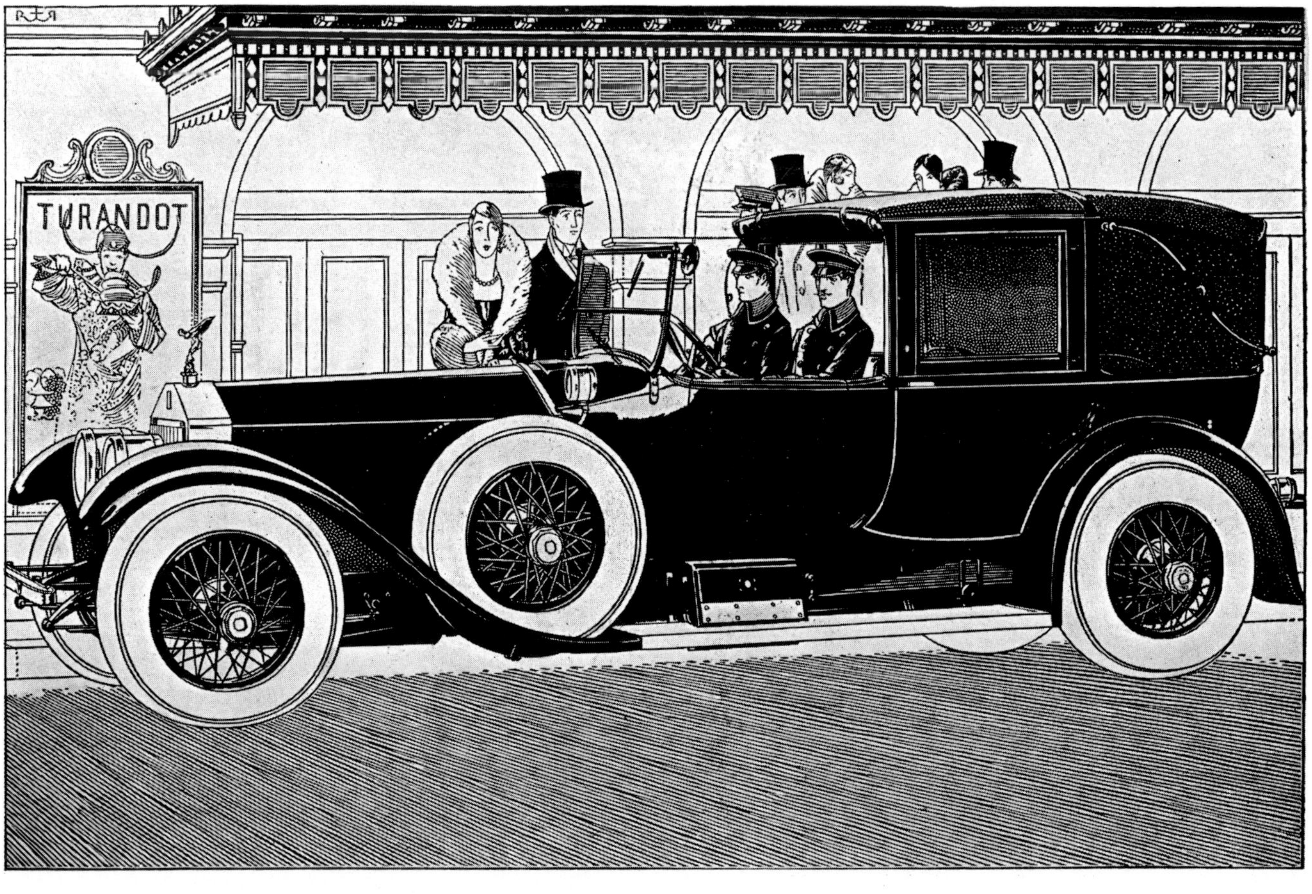

TURANDOT

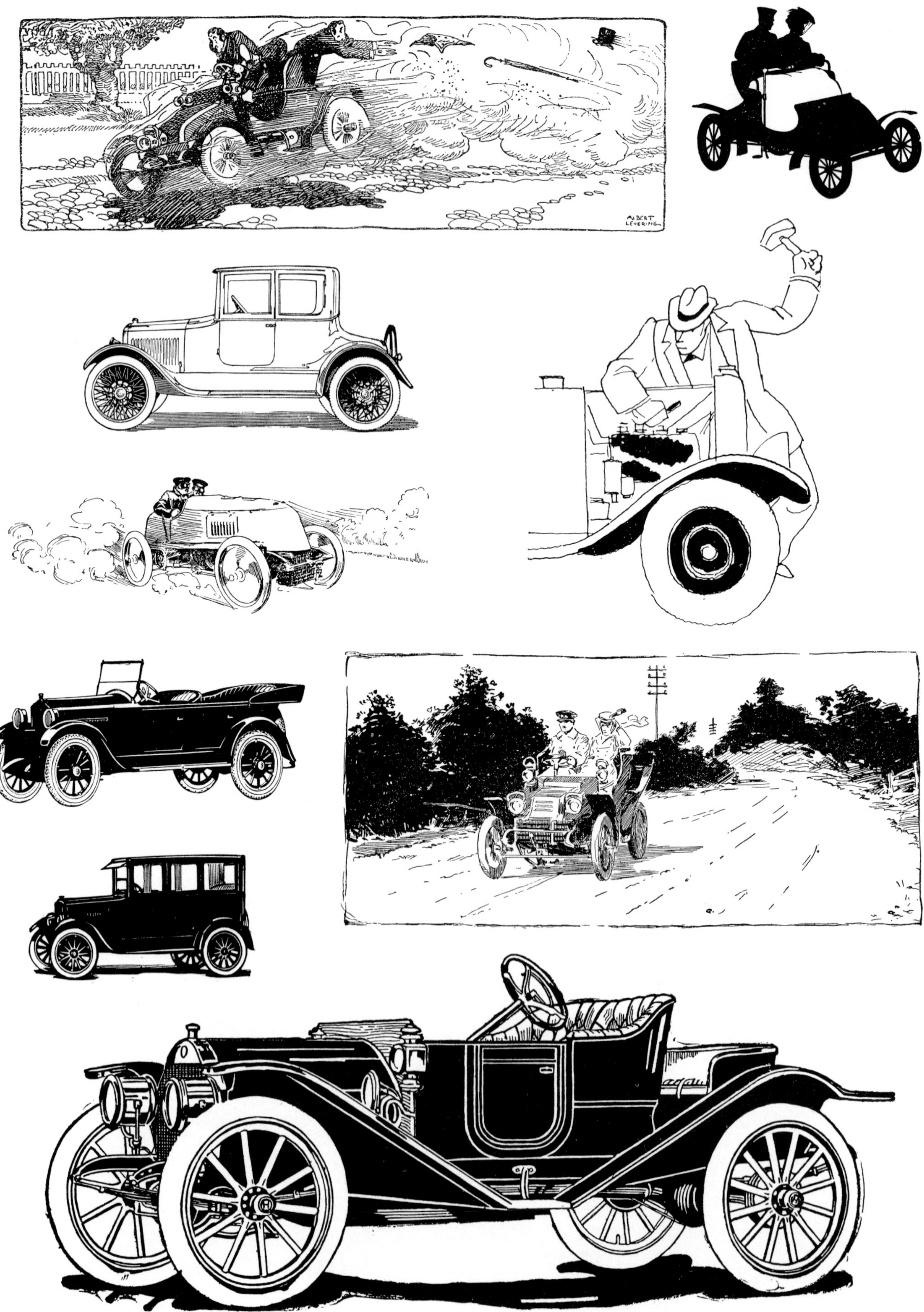
ALBERT
LEVERING

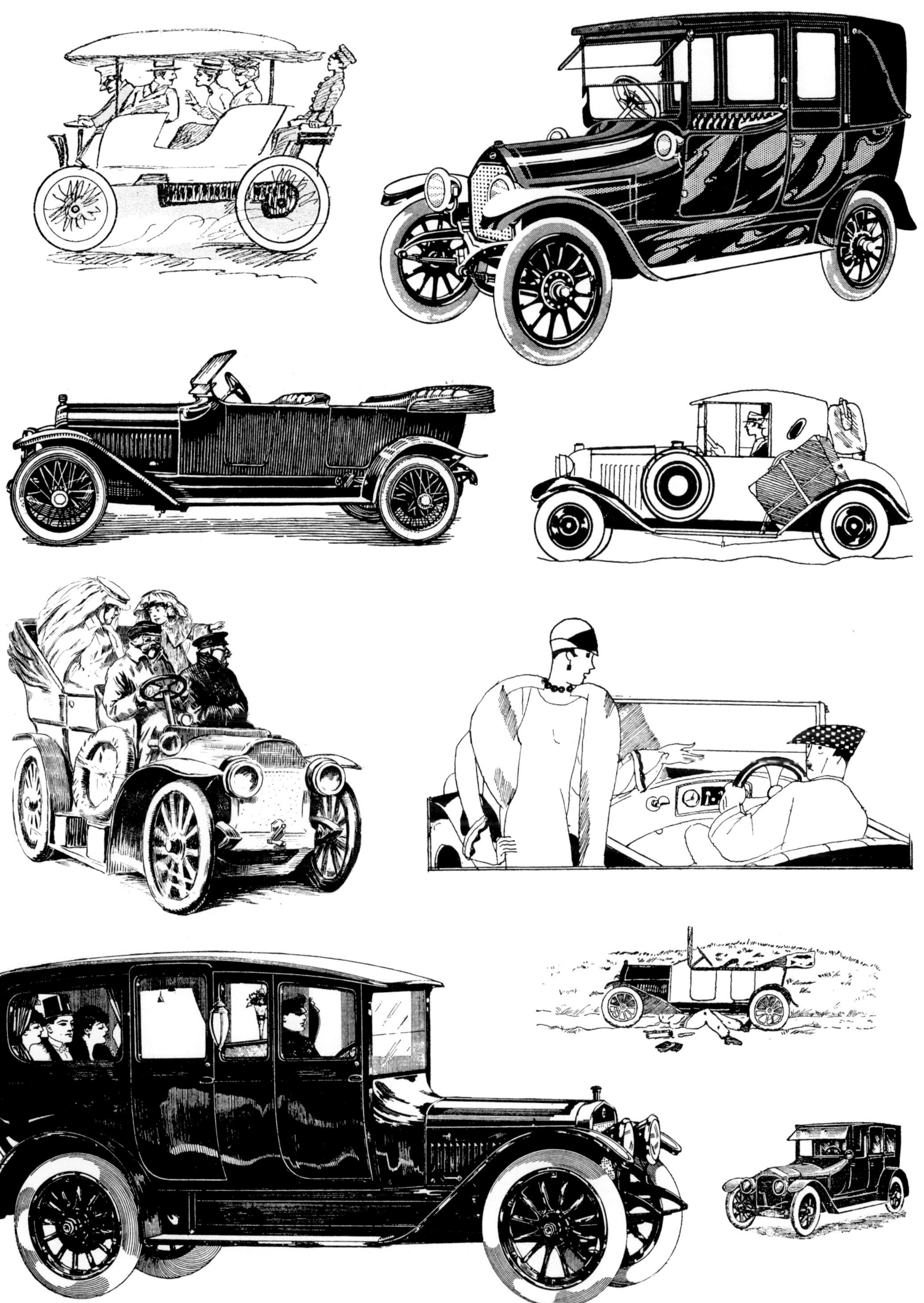

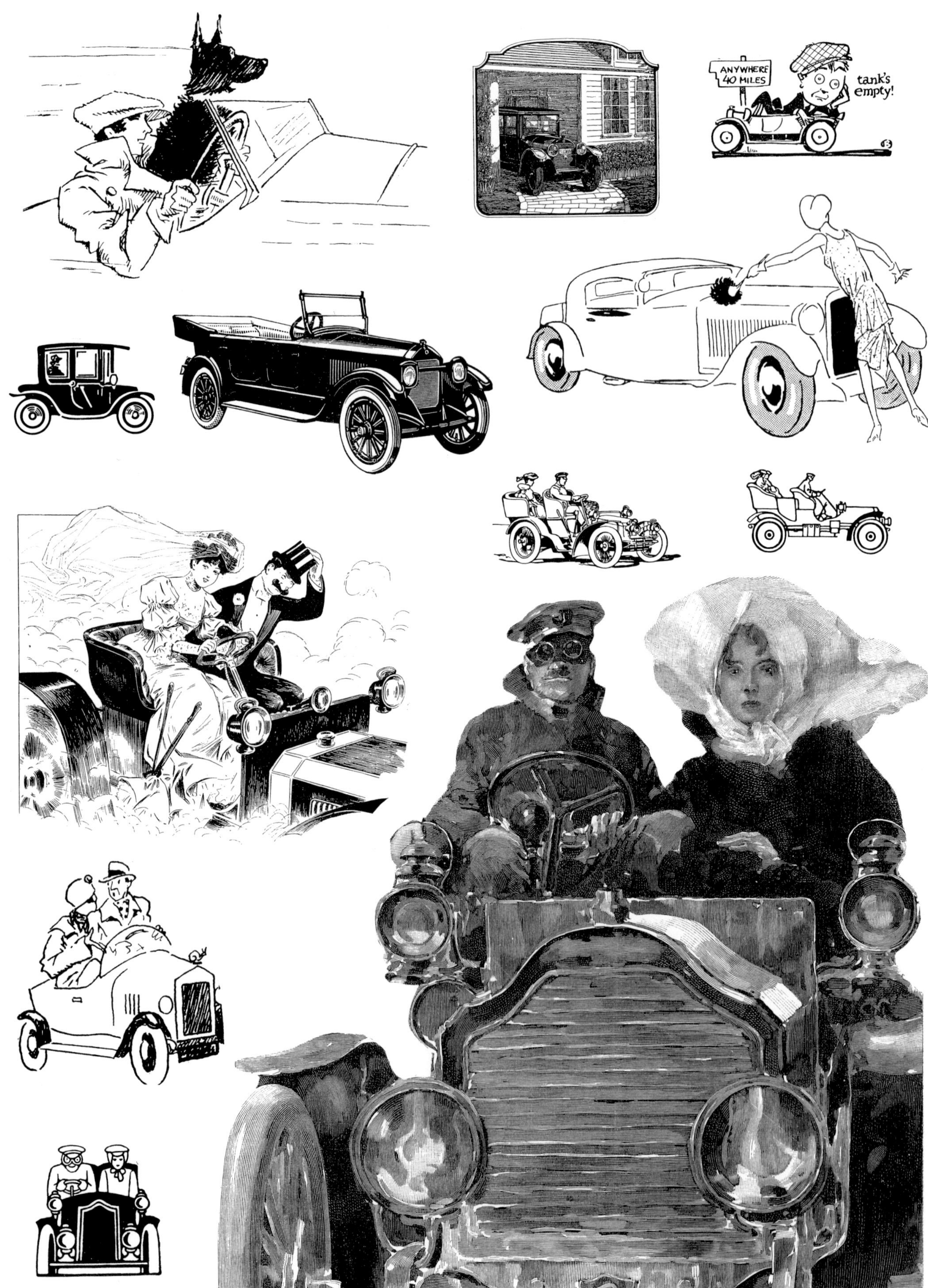
ANYWHERE
40 MILES
tank's
empty!

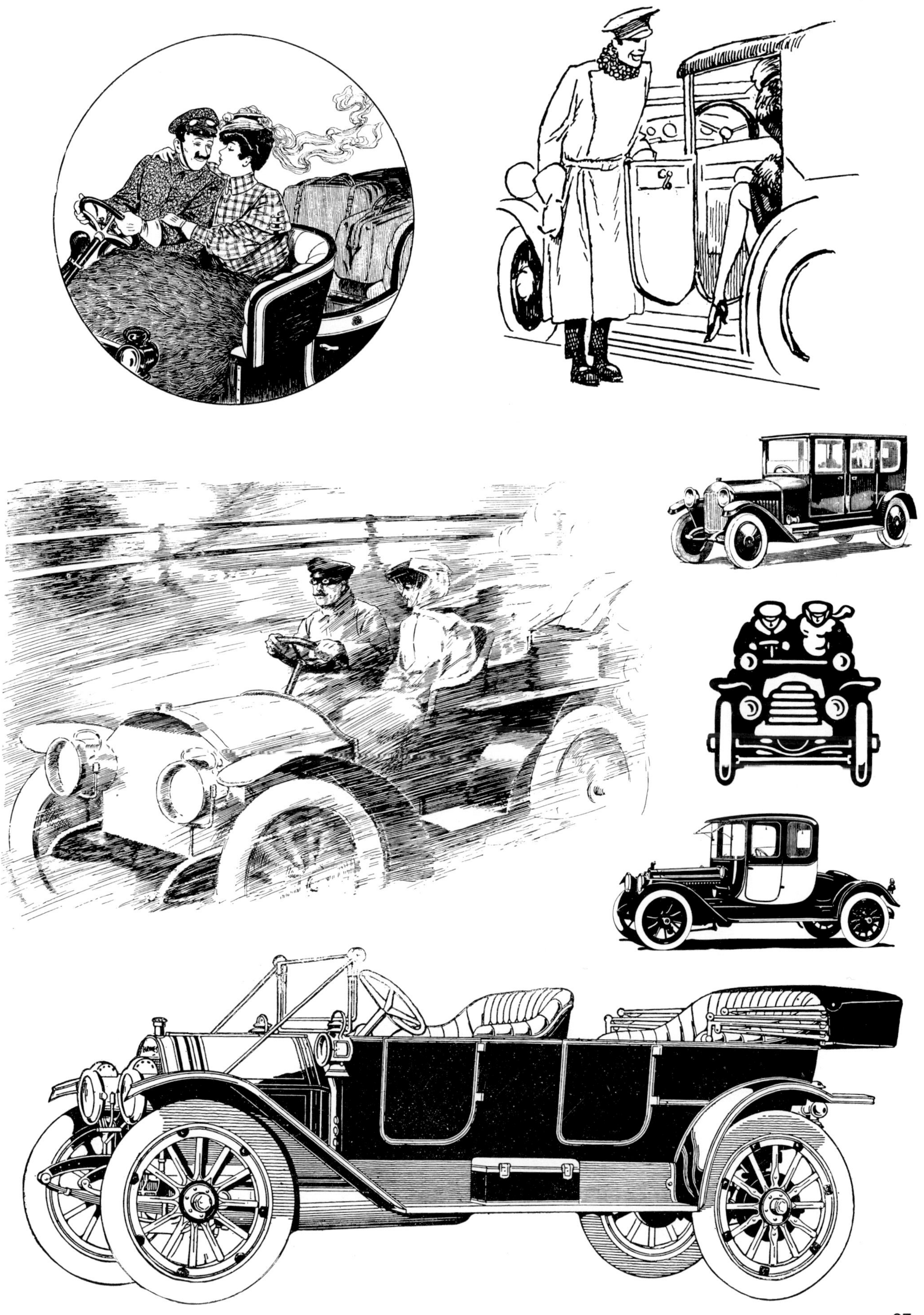

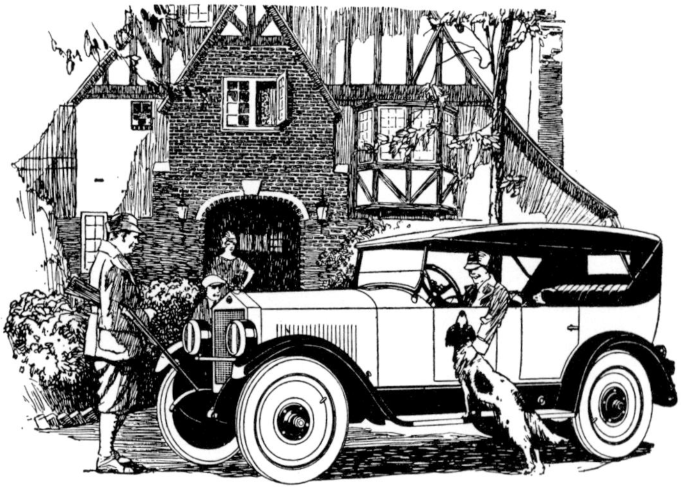

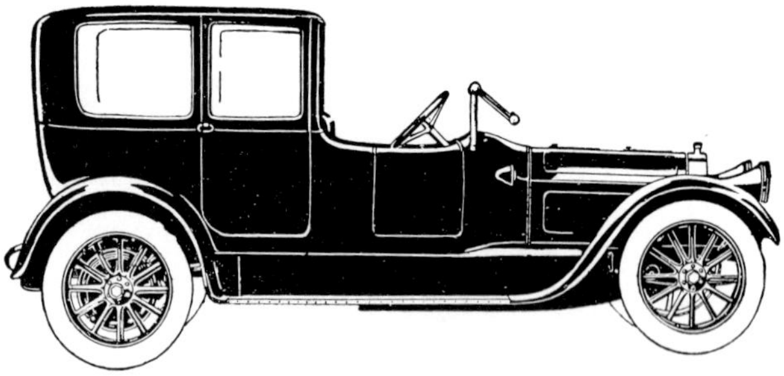

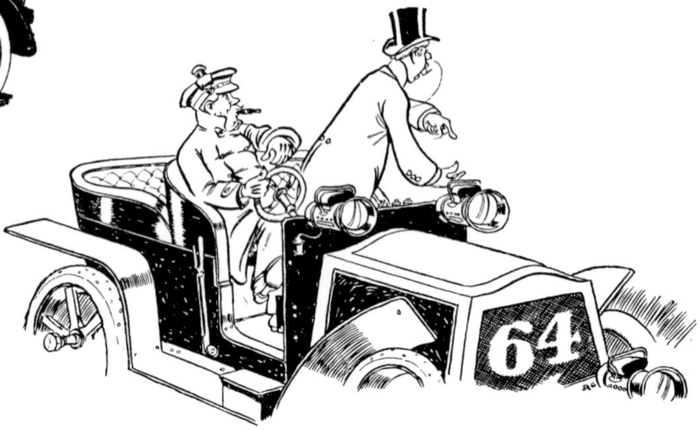

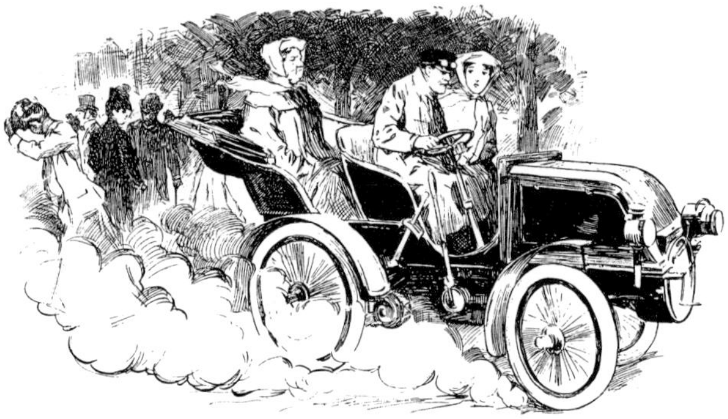

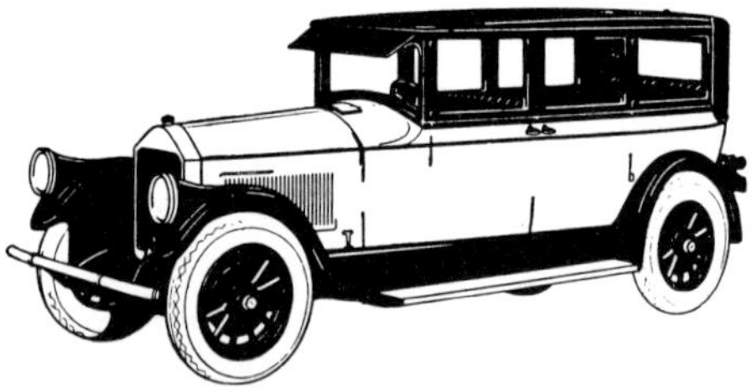

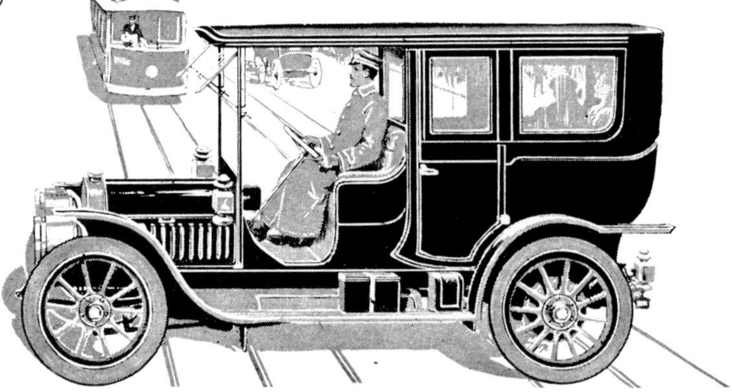

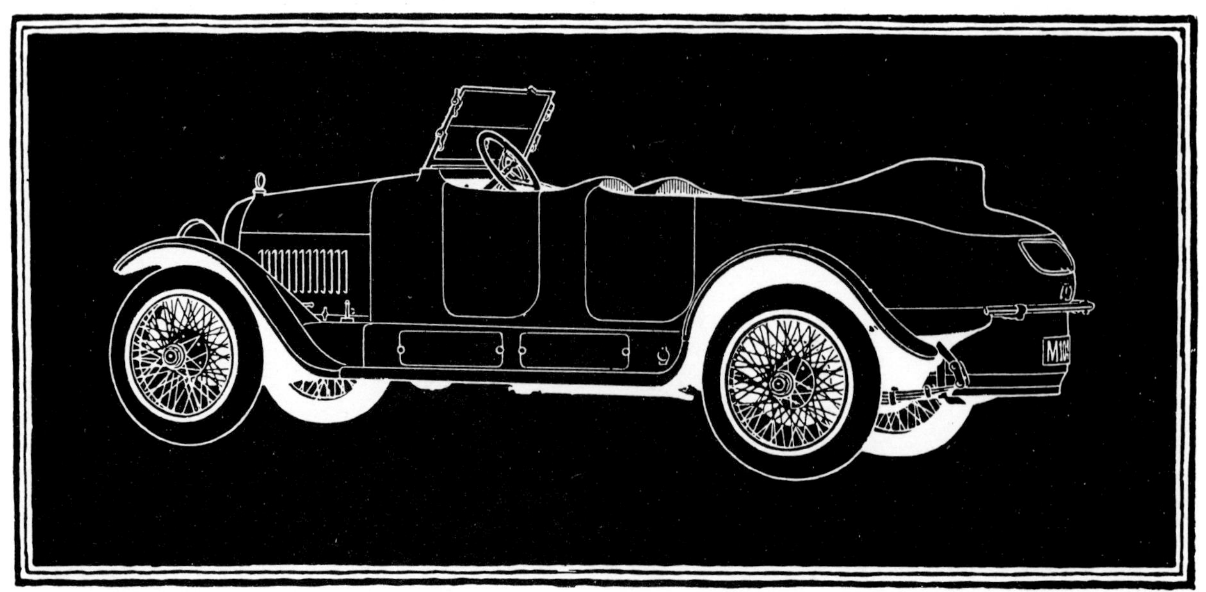

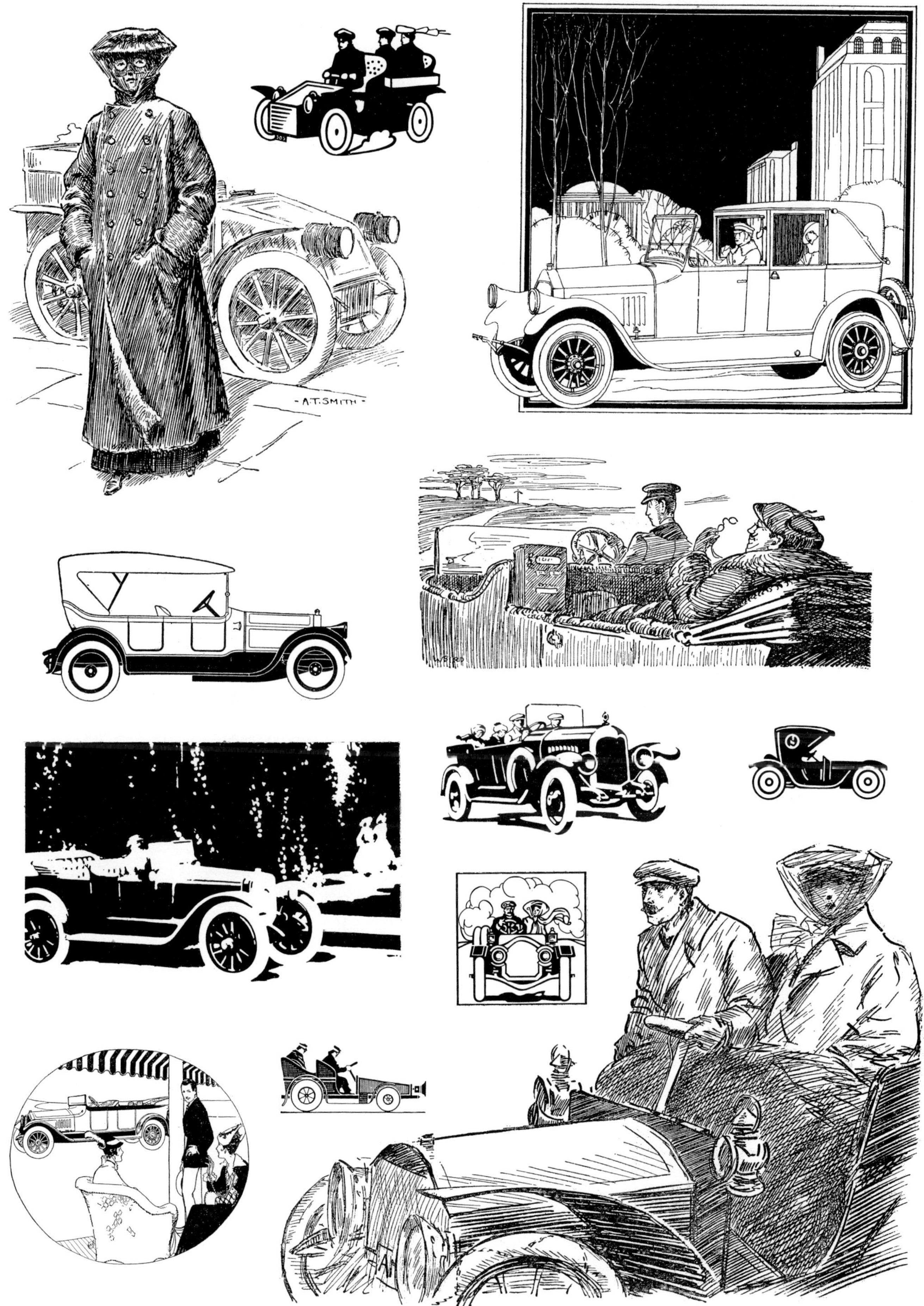

-A.T. SMITH-

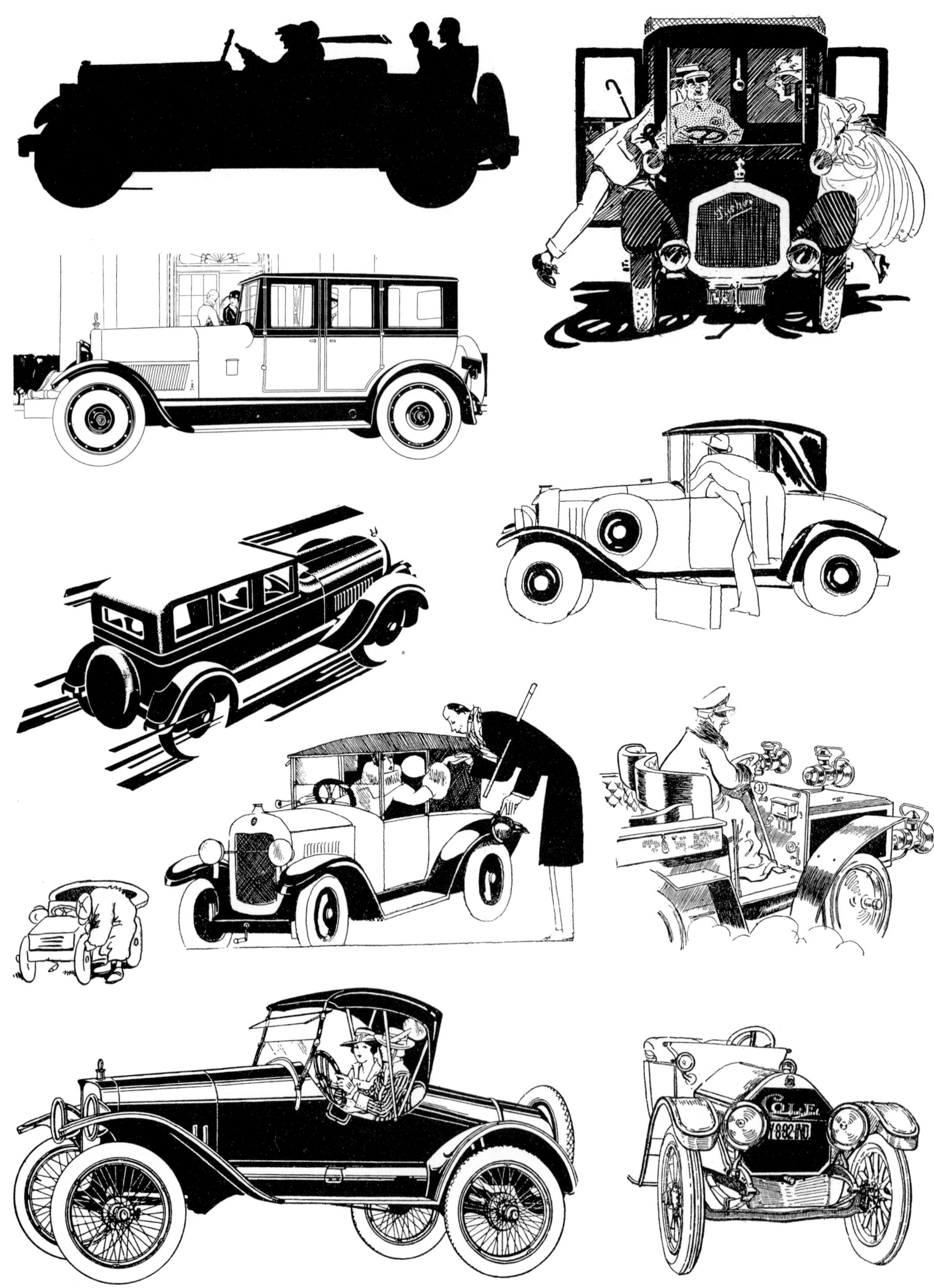

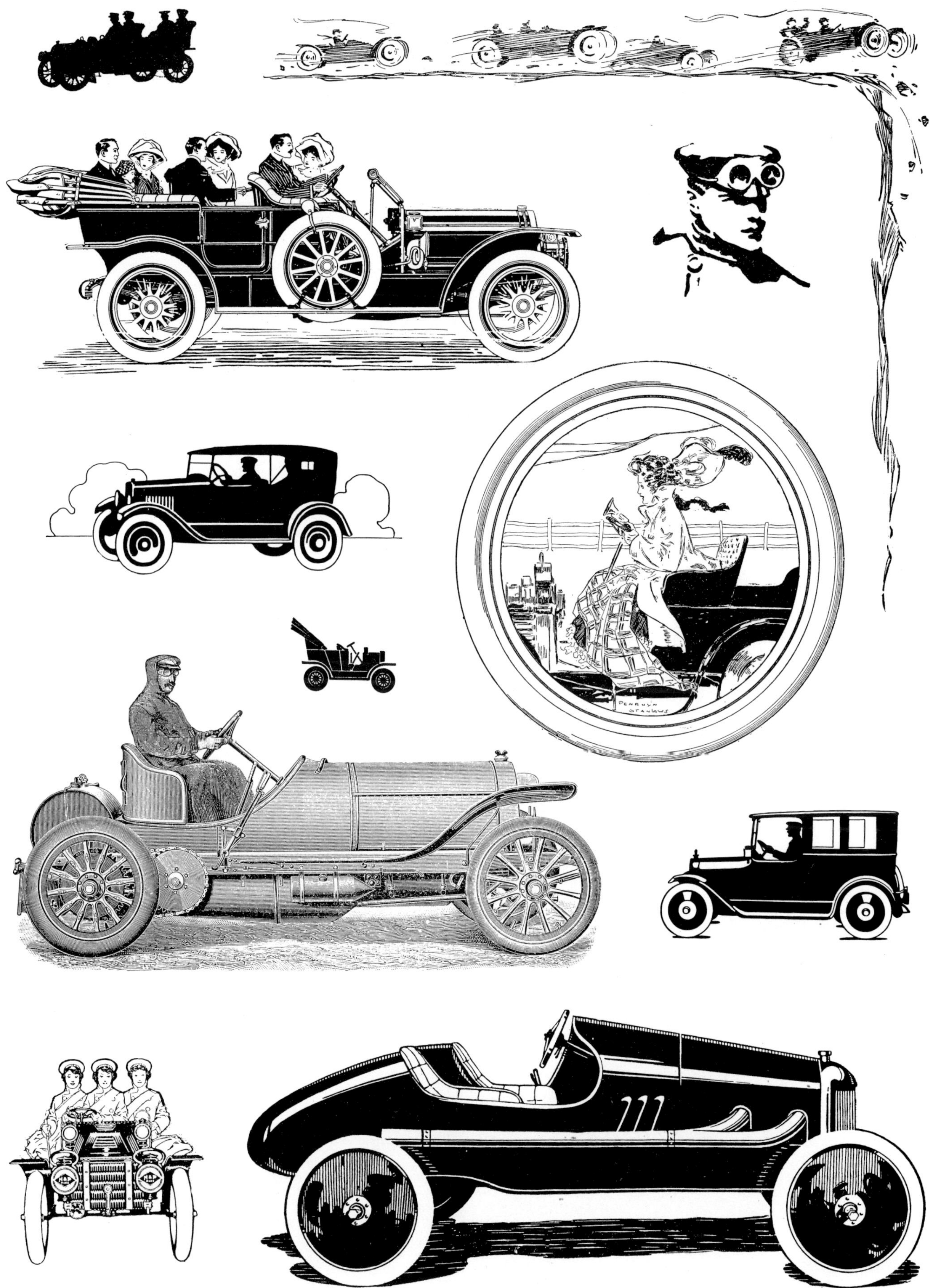
PENRHYN STANLAWS

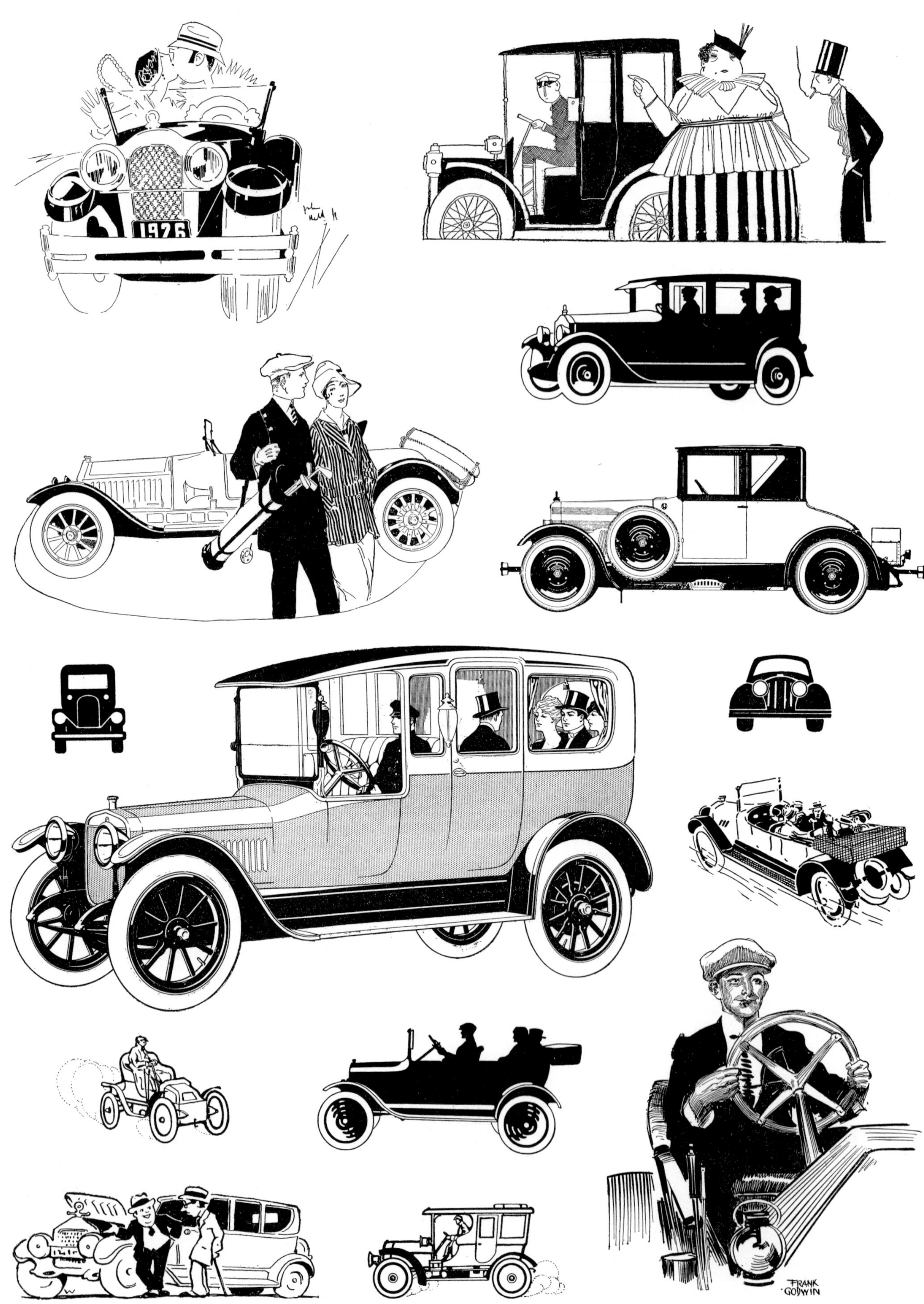
1926
FRANK GODWIN